7

ANGUS

GLENS

Advice to Readers

Readers are advised that whilst every effort is taken by the author to ensure the accuracy of this guidebook, changes can occur which may affect the contents. A book of this nature with specific descriptions is more prone to change than others. Waymarking alters, there may be new buildings or eradication of old buildings. It is advisable to check locally on transport, accommodation, shops etc but even rights-of-way can be altered and paths can be eradicated by landslip, forest fires or changes of ownership. The publisher would welcome notes of any such changes for future editions.

Safety Note

It is most important that walkers and cyclists take note of and adhere to signs erected by Forest Enterprise relating to timber harvesting operations which may occur throughout their forests. At all times cyclists should abide by the Mountain Bike Code.

THE ANGUS GLENS

A personal survey of the Angus Glens
for mountainbikers and walkers

by

Peter D Koch-Osborne

cp

CICERONE PRESS
MILNTHORPE CUMBRIA ENGLAND

© P. D. Koch-Osborne 1997
ISBN 1 85284 248 2

British Library Cataloguing-in-Publication Data.
A catalogue record for this book is
available from the British Library.

With tolerance and understanding
there is room for all of us who appreciate
and enjoy this very special environment.
                    —signpost, Glen Dye.

Cover pictures :- Glen Lee
                  Glen Muick

Index

5

Introduction

Access to the tracks on the following pages can rarely be regarded as an absolute right by the cyclist or walker. Almost all land is private and it is often only the good nature of the owners that allows us to travel unhindered over his land. In Scottish law the term trespass implies nuisance or damage. In practice sensible conduct removes any possibility of nuisance. Respect the grouse season (12 Aug to 10 Dec) and deer stalking (1 Jul to 20 Oct - stags and 21 Oct to 15 Feb - hinds). Your author has not once met with animosity in meeting 'keepers. Your good conduct will ensure continued access. Cyclists - stay on the trail and slow down!!

Conservation of the wild areas of Scotland is of paramount importance. Much has been written elsewhere but users of this guide must appreciate that the very ground over which you walk or cycle will be damaged if care is not taken. Please don't use a bike on soft peat paths and tread carefully on other than a stony track. Many of the tracks are in themselves an eyesore and any "development" can cause irreparable damage. Make sure, as walkers and cyclists, we encourage the conservation of our wilderness areas without the pressure of our activities causing further damage. In publishing this book a great deal of trust is placed upon you, the reader, to respect the needs of the region. If all you need is exercise - go to a sports centre! but if you appreciate the unique qualities of the wild places they are yours to enjoy..... carefully! Careless conduct not only damages what we seek to enjoy but, equally seriously, gives landowners good reason to restrict access.

The Maps on the following pages give sufficient detail for exploration of the glens but the Ordnance Survey Landranger maps of the region should also be used if the full geographical context of the area is to be fully appreciated. These maps and the knowledge of their proper use are essential if a long tour or cross country route is to be undertaken.

The mountain bike, or ATB - all terrain bike, has in the author's opinion been badly named. It does not belong on the high tops but is ideal in the glens covering at least twice the distance of the average walker, quietly, whilst still allowing a full appreciation of the surroundings and providing further exploration into the wilderness especially on short winter days. The bike must be a well maintained machine complete with a few essential spares as a broken bike miles from anywhere can be serious. Spare gear is best carried in strong panniers on good carriers. Poor quality bikes and accessories simply will not last. Front panniers help distribute weight and prevent "wheelies." Mud-guards are essential. Heavy rucksacks are tiring and put more weight onto one's already battered posterior! The brightly coloured "high profile" image of mountainbiking is unsuited to the remote glens. These wild areas are sacred and need treating as such.

Clothing for the mountainbiker is an important consideration, traditional road cycling gear is un-suitable. High ankle trainers are best for summer, and light weight walking boots for winter cycling. A zipped fleece jacket with waterproof top and overtrousers with spare thin sweatshirts etc should be included for easily adjusting temperature. The wearing of a helmet is a personal choice, it depends how you ride, where you ride and the value you place on your head! In any event a thin balaclava will be required under a helmet in winter or a thick one in place of a helmet. Good waterproof gloves are essential. Fingers and ears get painfully cold on a long descent at −5°C. Protection against exposure should be as for mountain walking. Many of the glens are as high as English hilltops. The road cyclist's shorts or longs will keep legs warm in summer only. In winter walker's breeches and overtrousers are more suitable.

<u>Clothing</u> for the walker has had much written about it elsewhere. Obviously full waterproofs, spare warm clothing, spare food etc. should be included. In winter conditions the longer through routes should never be attempted alone or by the inexperienced.

<u>Mountainbikers and walkers</u> alike should never be without a good map, this book (!), a whistle (and knowledge of its proper use), compass, emergency rations, and in winter a sleeping bag and cooker may be included even if an overnight stop is not planned. Word of your planned route should be left together with your estimated time of arrival. The bothies must be left tidy with firewood for the next visitor. Don't be too proud to remove someone else's litter. Join the Mountain Bothies Association to help support the maintenance of these simple shelters. It should not be necessary to repeat the Country Code and the Mountain Bike Code, the true lover of the wild places needs peace and space - not rules and regulations.

River crossings are a major consideration when planning long or "through" routes virtually anywhere in Scotland. It must be remembered that snowmelt from the high mountains can turn what is a fordable stream in early morning into a raging torrent by mid afternoon. Walkers should hold on to each other, in three's, forming a triangle if possible. Rivers can be easier to cross with a bike, as the bike can be moved, brakes applied, leant on, then the feet can be re-positioned and so on. The procedure is to remove boots and socks, replace boots, make sure you can't drop anything and cross - ouch! Drain boots well, dry your feet and hopefully your still dry socks will help to warm your feet up. Snowmelt is so cold it hurts. Choose a wide shallow point to cross and above all don't take risks.

Ascents on a bike should be tackled steadily in a very low gear and sitting down wherever possible. While front panniers prevent "wheelies" sitting down helps the rear wheel grip. Standing on the pedals causes wheel slip, erosion, and is tiring. Pushing a laden mountainbike is no fun and usually the result of tackling the lower half of a climb standing up, in the wrong gear or too fast.

Descents on a bike can be exhilarating but a fast descent is hard on the bike, the rider, and erodes the track if wheels are locked. It is also ill-mannered towards others who may be just around the next bend.

Last but not least other users of the tracks need treating with respect - it may be the owner! Bad conduct can only lead to restricted access, spoiling it for us all.

The Maps 1

The maps are drawn to depict the most important features to the explorer of the glens. North is always at the top of each map and all maps, apart from the detail sketches, are to the same scale :- 1km or 0.6 miles being shown on each map. An attempt has been made to present the maps in a pictorially interesting way. A brief explanation of the various features is set out below :-

<u>Tracks</u> :- One of the prime objects of this book is to grade the tracks according to "roughness". This information is essential to the mountainbiker and useful to the walker. With due respect to the Ordnance Survey one "other road, drive or track" can take twice as long to cycle along as another yet both may be depicted in the same way. The author's attempt at grading is set out below:-

metalled road, not too many fortunately, public roads are generally included only to locate the start of a route.

good track, hardly rutted, nearly as fast as a road to cycle on but can be boring to walk far on. Most are forest tracks.

the usual rutted "Landrover" track, rough but all easily rideable on a mountainbike, not too tedious to walk on.

rough, very rutted track nearly all rideable, can be very rough even for walking. Either very stony or overgrown or boggy.

walker's path, usually over 50% is rideable and included especially as a part of a through route. Details given on each map.

10

<u>Relief</u> is depicted in two ways. The heavy black lines are now a commonly used method of depicting main mountain summits, ridges and spurs thus:-

Contour lines are also used, at 50m intervals up to about 600m. This adds "shape" to the glens as mapped and gives the reader an idea of how much climbing is involved. Reference to the gradient profiles at the start of each section compares the various routes:-

$$\underline{500}_m \qquad \underline{550}_m \qquad \underline{600}_m$$

<u>Crags</u> in the high mountains are shown thus:-
....with major areas of scree shown dotted

<u>Rivers</u> generally "uncrossable" are shown as two lines whilst streams, generally "crossable" are shown using a single line. Note:- great care is needed crossing even the larger streams.
Falling in can cause embarrassment at best, exposure or drowning at worst. Please don't take risks - besides you'd get this book wet !!

loch or lochan

<u>Buildings</u> and significant ruins are shown as a:-■

<u>Bridges</u> are rather obviously shown thus:-
There are so many trees I wish there were an easier way of drawing them but there isn't! I'm fed up with drawing trees!!

etc etc.....

11

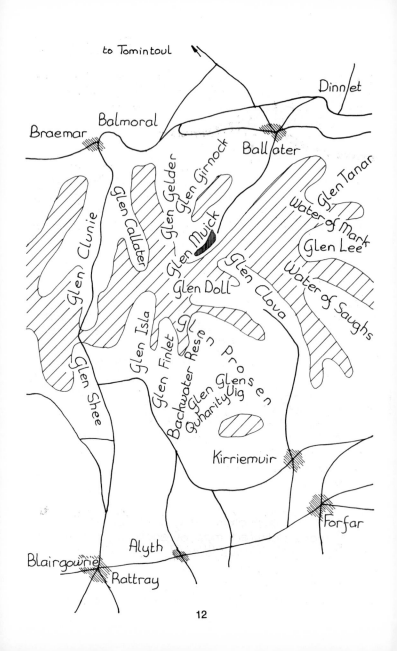

to Tomintoul

Dinnet

Braemar Balmoral

Ballater

Glen Clunie

Glen Callater

Glen Gelder

Glen Girnock

Glen Muick

Glen Tanar

Water of Mark

Glen Lee

Water of Saughs

Glen Doll

Glen Clova

Glen Isla

Glen Finlet

Backwater Resr.

Glen Prosen

Glen Glensen

Quharity Uig

Glen Shee

Kirriemuir

Forfar

Blairgowrie

Alyth

Rattray

12

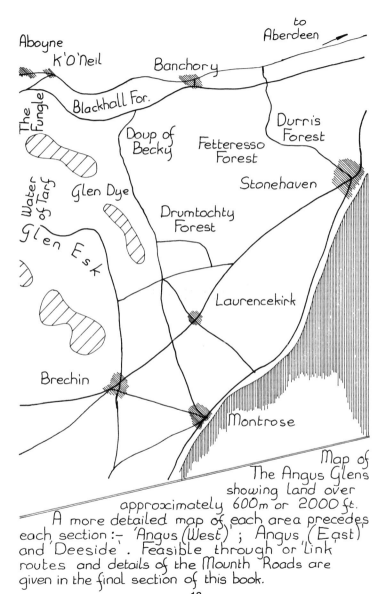

Map of
The Angus Glens
showing land over
approximately 600m or 2000 ft.

A more detailed map of each area precedes each section :- 'Angus (West)'; Angus (East) and 'Deeside'. Feasible through or 'Link' routes and details of the 'Mounth' Roads are given in the final section of this book.

13

Angus (West)

Angus (West)

Access:- The area is bordered to the west by the A93 Cairnwell road (the old 'Devil's Elbow) over to Braemar from Glen Shee. To the south lies a pleasant collection of cycle-friendly 'B' and minor roads which lie north of the Rattray to Kirriemuir main road. Access is rapid from both Perth and Dundee. For cyclists, the quiet glen (public) roads are worth traversing as a prelude to the off-road glen tracks given in the following pages. Access to the north and east is only by the Mounth Roads - ancient drove roads - now hillwalkers' paths from Deeside to Strathmore, not cycle routes.

Accommodation:- Apart from the ideally situated Glen Doll Youth Hostel - in the heart of the region - accommodation is sparse north of Dunkeld, Blairgowrie and Kirriemuir, all of which have tourist information centres. (Only Blairgowrie is open all year.) Here also are facilities for caravans and camping. The tourist is generally well catered for in this region with numerous car parks, information panels, loos (!) etc., a result of the proximity of the population centres of Perth and Dundee to the scenic delights of the glens.

Geographical Features :— The Lochnagar plateau is often included in the Cairngorm region and the nature of these mountains is certainly similar to the Cairngorms 'proper'; high plateau, with rounded tops but deep and dramatic corries abound. The high mountain scene gives way to moor, then forest and hill sheep country as one travels south, the lower land being dissected by the picturesque glens covered in detail in this section.

Mountains :- Lochnagar reigns supreme (and

really belongs to Deeside) but the lesser heights of Broad-Cairn, Glas Maol and Mayar together with numerous 3000-foot-plus tops provide the truly wild heart of the region. This is, in winter, ski-mountaineering country; in summer an area just asking for those long sorties into the hills only the summer daylight hours will allow.

Rivers:- Water drains south to the Tay from Glen Isla, Glen Finlet, Backwater Reservoir and Glen Quharity; whilst Glen Uig, Glen Doll, Glen Clova and Glen Prosen drain into the River South Esk, bound for Montrose. The River Isla becomes a major tributary of the Tay but there are no problems with river crossings in the upper glens.

Forests:- Glen Isla Forest, occupying Glen Finlet is the largest, whilst Glenclova Forest lies awkwardly in Glen Prosen. Glen Doll Forest is (surprisingly!) actually in Glen Doll although this does extend into Glen Clova. Why are these forests named after the adjacent glen? It is all very confusing! Sadly there are no significant areas of natural woodland.

Lochs:- None, other than the dammed Backwater Reservoir, and a little to the south the Loch of Lintrathen which is a nature reserve despite being closely encircled by a public road.

Emergency:- The glen routes are generally tame and start from populated areas. However many of these run on to become serious hill (walking, not cycling) routes and should be treated as such regarding equipment, clothing and experience. Whilst an inviting hill track begs exploration, unless properly planned with ample time allowed poor weather can turn a day out into an epic - or worse! The Glen Doll Youth Hostel is a mountain rescue post.

Angus (West) Routes 1

Glen Isla

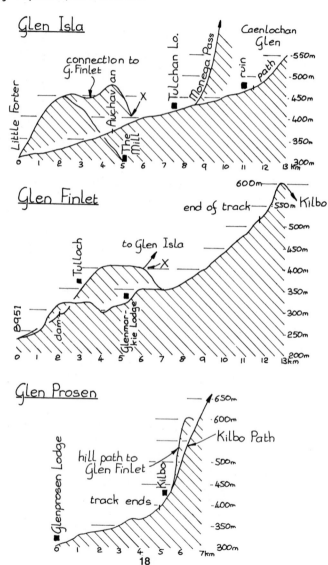

connection to G. Finlet

Little Forter

Auchavan

X

The Mill

Tulchan Lo.

Monega Pass

Caenlochan Glen

ruin

path

-550m
-500m
-450m
-400m
-350m
-300m

0 1 2 3 4 5 6 7 8 9 10 11 12 13 Km

Glen Finlet

600m

end of track

Kilbo

to Glen Isla

X

550m
-500m
-450m
-400m
-350m
-300m
-250m
-200m

Tulloch

B951

dam

Glenmarkie Lodge

0 1 2 3 4 5 6 7 8 9 10 11 12 13km

Glen Prosen

-650m
-600m

Kilbo Path

hill path to Glen Finlet

Kilbo

-500m
-450m

track ends

-400m
-350m
-300m

Glenprosen Lodge

0 1 2 3 4 5 6 7km

18

Glen Quharity/Glen Uig

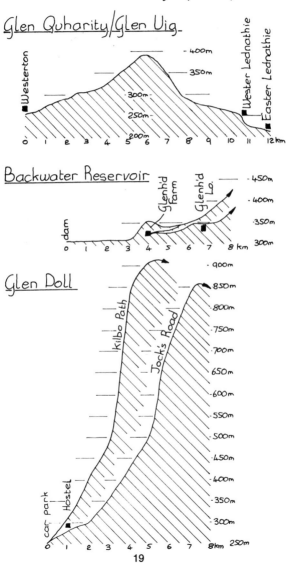

Backwater Reservoir

Glen Doll

Angus (West) Routes 3

Glen Clova

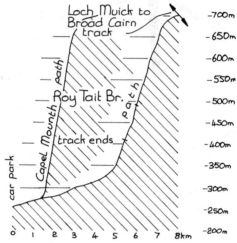

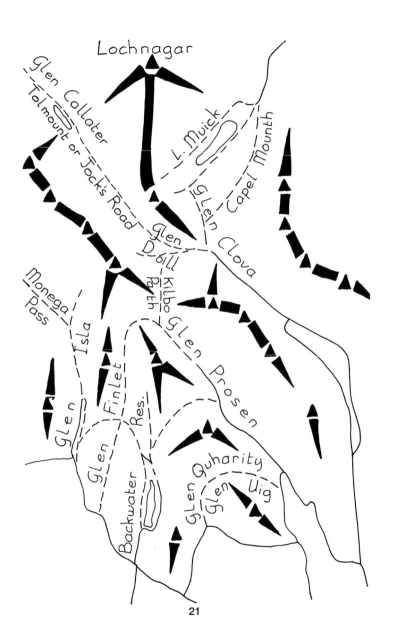

Lochnagar

Glen Callater

Tolmount or Jock's Road

L. Muick

Capel Mounth

Glen Doll

Glen Clova

Monega Pass

Kilbo Path

Glen Isla

Glen Finlet

Glen Prosen

Backwater Res.

Glen Quharity

Glen Uig

Glb

21

Glen Isla 1

This section covers the true head of Glen Isla, not the Glen Isla Forest as named by Forest Enterprise - this is Glen Finlet. Confused? So am I!! Glen Isla comprises the 'lower' glen with quiet public road and an interesting old road, now a track; an upper section to the glen head; a hill path to Glen Clunie via the Monega Pass; and a connection to Glen Finlet leading in turn to both Backwater Reservoir and Glen Prosen. The distance from Folda to the ruin at the head of Glen Isla is about 12km or 7·5 miles one way. Glen Isla may be part of a long distance cross-country walk, a short ramble or a day on the bike using the public road and the loop around Auchintaple Loch to The Mill. There is, however no shelter.

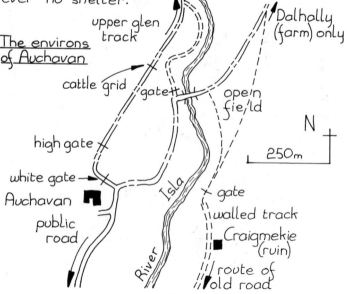

The environs of Auchavan

upper glen track

cattle grid

Dalhally (farm) only

gate

open field

N

250m

high gate

white gate

Auchavan

public road

Isla

gate

walled track

Craigmekie (ruin)

route of old road

River Isla

N+

1 km

↑Continued Glen Isla 3↑

664 m

658 m

gate

500

Balandun
Hill

Fergus

740m

350

ford and
footbr.

gates

450

Dail na
Sneachd

400

350

old
"road"

Continued Glen Finlet 2↑

400

ford

views ↑↑

R. Isla

gates

gates

rusty shed

Little Forter

high
gate

high
gte.

private

high
gate

Auchintaple
Loch

to
Glenshee

Castle

Folda

dam

400

Craighead

R. Isla

The final 1km section of
the connection to Glen
Finlet is very rough.

gate
The Mill

350

to Kirriemuir

400

23

Glen Isla 3

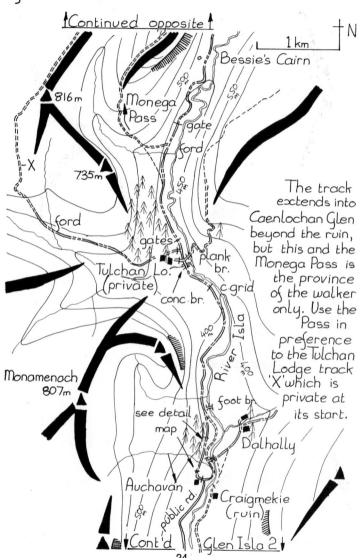

1 km

N

Bessie's Cairn

816 m

Monega Pass

gate

ford

X

735m

ford

gates

plank br.

Tulchan Lo. (private)

c. grid

conc. br.

The track extends into Caenlochan Glen beyond the ruin, but this and the Monega Pass is the province of the walker only. Use the Pass in preference to the Tulchan Lodge track 'X' which is private at its start.

Monamenoch 807m

River Isla

foot br.

see detail map

Dalhally

Auchavan

public rd.

Craigmekie (ruin)

↓Cont'd

Glen Isla 2 ↓

24

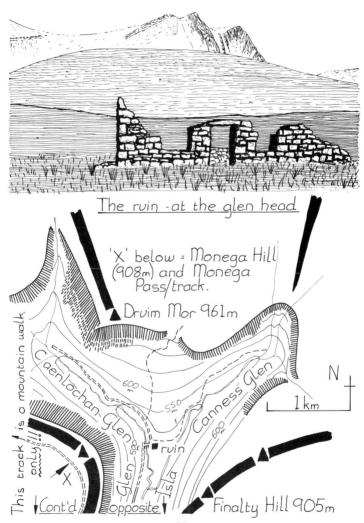

The ruin - at the glen head

'X' below = Monega Hill (908m) and Monega Pass/track.

▲ Druim Mor 961m

Caenlochan Glen

600

550

N

1 km

This track is a mountain walk only!!!

Glen Isla

Canness Glen

600

ruin

←Cont'd   opposite↓

▲ Finalty Hill 905m

X

25

Glen Finlet 1

Glen Finlet is known, according to Forest Enterprise, as Glen Isla Forest. It is well connected,
having links to Glen Isla, Backwater Reservoir,
and the head of Glen Prosen. A further path
runs out to the mid-point of Glen Prosen. Only
the links to Glen Isla and Backwater Resr.
are feasible with a bike. Feasible that is....
neither would be listed in your author's "ten
best cycle rides"! The Glen Finlet tracks
provide a good day out on the bike and offer
the walker numerous options. Cyclists should
keep off the purpose-made ski trails as these
are (obviously) unsurfaced.

Glenmarkie Lodge

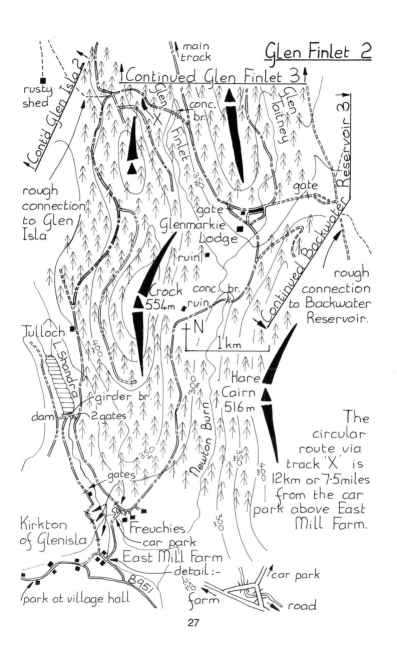

main track

↑Continued Glen Finlet 3↑

Cont'd Glen Isla 2

rusty shed

Glen Finlet

conc. br.

Glen Taitney

Continued Backwater Reservoir 3

rough connection to Glen Isla

gate

gate

Glenmarkie Lodge

ruin

Crock 554m

conc. br.

ruin

rough connection to Backwater Reservoir.

+N

1km

Tulloch

L. Shandra

400 350

dam

girder br.

2 gates

gates

Newton Burn

300

Hare Cairn 516m

350

300

400

300

The circular route via track 'X' is 12km or 7.5miles from the car park above East Mill Farm.

Kirkton of Glenisla

Freuchies car park

East Mill Farm detail:-

B951

park at village hall

car park

farm

road

250

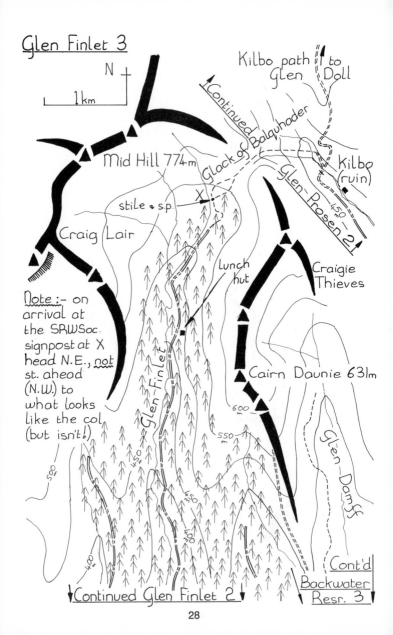

Glen Finlet 3

N

1km

Kilbo path to Glen Doll

Continued Balquhader

Continued

Mid Hill 774m

Glack of Balquhader

Kilbo (ruin)

stile • s.p.

X

Glen Prosen 2

450

Craig Lair

Lunch hut

Craigie Thieves

Note :- on arrival at the SRWSoc. signpost at X head N.E., not st. ahead (N.W.) to what looks like the col (but isn't!)

Glen Finlet

Cairn Daunie 631m

600

550

Glen Damff

500

450

450

450

400

Continued Glen Finlet 2

Cont'd Backwater Resr. 3

Glen Prosen boasts only a short track from the end of the public road to the ruin at Kilbo. The one-way distance is a mere 5·5km or 3·5miles. It is either a pleasant, if unremarkable walk, or cycle ride if ridden from Kirriemuir or Dykehead (28km/17·5m or 20km/12·5m respectively one way). The head of the glen has, however, strategic importance as Kilbo is almost passed en-route from Glen Finlet to Glen Doll, the path to the latter being named after the ruined cottage. There is nothing to be gained in pursuing the forest roads north, or the rough hill track up Lick. There is no shelter.

Glenclova Forest

Continued Glen Prosen 2

conc. br.
gate
400

Old Craig

350 m

footbridge
to nowhere

Lkd gate

Glenprosen Lodge

Bruntshields ▲
532m

hut

gates

gates

400
350

c. grids

N

450

park

300

1 km

Glen Prosen public road

Hill of Strone ▲ 512m

Glen Prosen 2

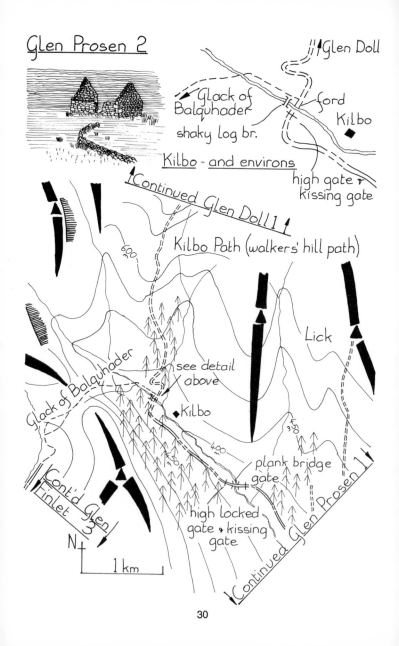

Glen Doll

Glack of Balquhader

shaky log br.

ford

Kilbo

Kilbo — and environs

high gate &
kissing gate

↑ Continued Glen Doll 1 ↑

Kilbo Path (walkers' hill path)

600

Lick

Glack of Balquhader

see detail above

◆ Kilbo

400

Cont'd Glen 3 Inlet

plank bridge
gate

high locked
gate & kissing
gate

N ↑

1 km

Continued Glen Prosen 1 ↗

Glen Quharity/Glen Uig 1

The Glen Quharity to Glen Uig track explores a delightful, almost secretive glen, which twists and turns its way from Balintore to Easter Lednathie in Glen Prosen, a distance of some 12km or 7·5 miles. For walkers, transport will be required at both ends but cyclists may complete the circuit on minor roads, frustratingly needing no less than three O.S. maps for the 26km/16·5 mile circuit. There is no shelter. Half a day should suffice for either the suggested walk or the circuit on a bike. A route probably best avoided during both lambing and grouse shooting seasons.

N

1 km

Continued Glen Quharity/Glen Uig 2

sm. ford

gate

Longdrum

300

350

Hill of Shanks 484m

plank bridges

c. grid

pl. bridge

Tombay 377m

Westerton

400

350

Quharity Burn

Balintore

Castle

'circuit'

250

To complete the anti-clockwise 'circuit' from Balintore Castle; turn left after 7km/4·5m, and left again at the 'phone box after a further 1km/0·75m. Continue N. a hilly 7km/4·5m to Easter Lednathie.

31

Glen Quharity/Glen Uig 2

To complete the clockwise 'circuit' from Easter Lednathie, turn right after 7km/4·5m (at the 'phone box), then right again after a further 1km/0·75m. Continue W. 7km/4·5m to Balintore.

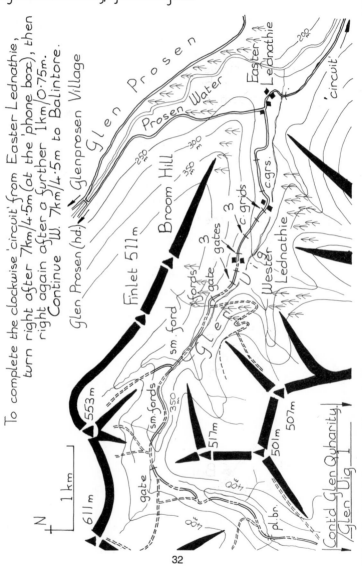

The numerous tracks and paths around, and north of Backwater Reservoir are more suitable for walkers than cyclists as most run out into rough paths in the upper glen. However it is possible to encircle the reservoir on a bike, via Barny, starting and finishing at the dam car park. The Link to Glen Finlet is also feasible by bike. The potential for those on foot extends to the interesting paths over the Glack of Barny and the Moss of Glanny. A hill path also exists to Cormuir— a couple of miles from the head of the Glen Prosen public road. Distance is very much to choice. Glenhead Farm is sheep territory so care at lambing time and leave the dog behind!

The complicated bit between Glenhead Farm and the connection to Glen Finlet is set out below to a larger scale:—

high gate

hill paths

link to Glen Finlet footbr.

gts.

Meikle Barny ▲

fence (no gates)

Glack of Barny

Moss of Glanny

vague

Little Barny ▲

|250m|

Cuilt Hill 477m ▲

track follows top edge of fields

Barny ◆

gate

to Glenhead Lodge

gate

gates

gates ◆ (Glendam)

gate

gate

public rd.

Glenhead Farm

33

Backwater Reservoir 2

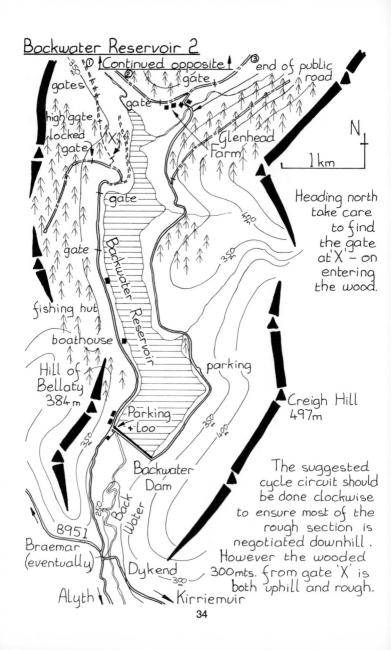

Continued opposite

end of public road

gates

gate

gate

high gate

locked gate

'X'

Glenhead Farm

gate

N

1 km

gate

Heading north take care to find the gate at 'X' – on entering the wood.

Backwater Reservoir

400

350

fishing hut

boathouse

parking

Hill of Bellaty 384 m

350

400

Parking + Loo

Creigh Hill 497m

Backwater Dam

350

250

The suggested cycle circuit should be done clockwise to ensure most of the rough section is negotiated downhill. However the wooded 300mts. from gate 'X' is both uphill and rough.

B951

Braemar (eventually)

Back Water

Dykend

300

Alyth

Kirriemuir

N

1km

Y

Cairn Daunie
631m

610m

W

X

524m

500m

450
350

Glen Damff

Glen Taitney

Continued Glen Finlet 2

Black
Binks
504m

400

350

A

Moss of Glanny

400

fords

B

gts.

450
350
350

① ② ③ gate

Cuilt
Hill
477m

gate

Z

gts.
400m

Glenhead Lodge

The rough paths W, X, + Y
run out to the hills
whilst Z continues
to Cormuir in Glen
Prosen. The path
'A' over the Glack
of Barny is a delight
and can be combined
with the Moss of
Glanny to form a
circular walk.
See detail on
B'wtr. Res. 1.

B is the
furthest point
of the only
practicable
cycle circuit.

Continued opposite

35

Glen Doll 1

↑Continued Glen Callater 4↑

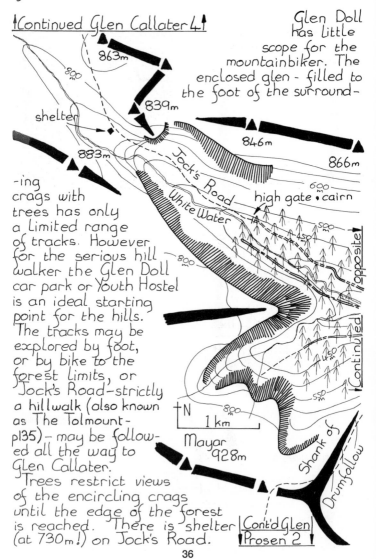

Glen Doll has little scope for the mountainbiker. The enclosed glen - filled to the foot of the surround-

863m

839m

shelter

846m

866m

883m

Jock's Road

White Water

high gate • cairn

600m

500m

450m

-ing crags with trees has only a limited range of tracks. However for the serious hill walker the Glen Doll car park or Youth Hostel is an ideal starting point for the hills. The tracks may be explored by foot, or by bike to the forest limits, or Jock's Road—strictly a hillwalk (also known as The Tolmount–p135) – may be followed all the way to Glen Callater. Trees restrict views of the encircling crags until the edge of the forest is reached. There is shelter (at 730m!) on Jock's Road.

800

450m

500m

↑N

1 km

Mayar 928m

Shank of Drumfollow

↓Continued IA opposite↓

↓Cont'd Glen Prosen 2↓

The complexities at the start are explained by signpost.

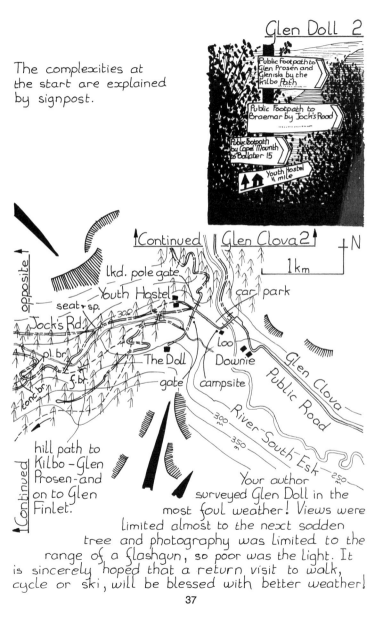

Glen Doll 2

Public Footpath to Glen Prosen and Glenisla by the Kilbo Path

Public Footpath to Braemar by Jock's Road

Public Footpath by Capel Mounth to Ballater 15

Youth Hostel ¼ mile

opposite ↑

↑Continued | Glen Clova 2↑ | ↑N

1 km

lkd. pole gate

Youth Hostel

car park

seat sp.

Jock's Rd.

300

loo

Glen Clova Public Road

pl. br

The Doll

Downie

f. br.

gate

campsite

conc. br

River South Esk

300
350 m
250

Continued ↓

hill path to Kilbo – Glen Prosen – and on to Glen Finlet.

Your author surveyed Glen Doll in the most foul weather! Views were limited almost to the next sodden tree and photography was limited to the range of a flashgun, so poor was the light. It is sincerely hoped that a return visit to walk, cycle or ski, will be blessed with better weather!

37

Glen Clova 1

Glen Clova offers slightly more scope than Glen Doll with a bike. Indeed, the close proximity of both glens allows half a day to be spent in each. The Glen Clova track degenerates into a rough walkers' path before the Tait bridge, from which a surprisingly short walk brings one to the shelter under Broad Cairn and a track which originates in Glen Muick. This connection is however no bike ride! The "reasonably ride-able" one-way distance from the car park is about 5km/3·5 miles, the Tait bridge being 6km or 4miles and the Broad Cairn track some 8km or just under 6miles from the start. There is no shelter - your author got wet again!!

Roy Tait
Memorial Bridge

The memorial plaque.
Don't fall down the
waterfall trying to
read it!... it's in
a daft place!!

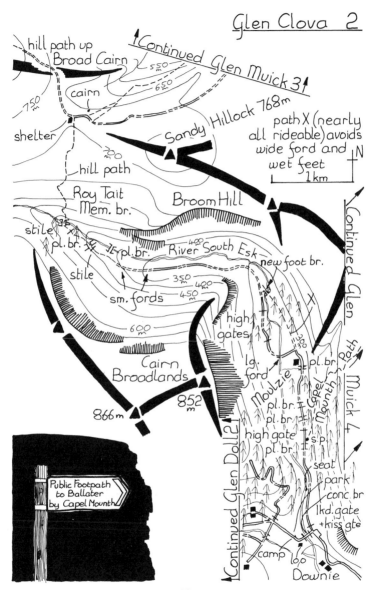

hill path up
Broad Cairn

Continued Glen Muick 3

cairn

shelter

hill path

Sandy Hillock 768m

path X (nearly
all rideable) avoids
wide ford and
wet feet

N

1 km

Roy Tait
Mem. br.

Broom Hill

stile

pl. br.

pl. br.

River South Esk

new foot br.

Continued Glen

stile

sm. fords

high
gates

Cairn
Broadlands

lg.
ford

Moulzie

pl. br.

Capel Mounth

pl. br.

Muick 4

866 m

852 m

high gate

pl. br.

s.p.

seat

park

conc. br

lkd. gate
+ kiss gate

Public Footpath
to Ballater
by Capel Mounth

Continued Glen Doll 2

camp

Downie

Angus (East)

Angus (East)

Access:— This area lies north west of the main A94 road to Stonehaven and thence, via the A92, to Aberdeen. The eastern section of the A93 Deeside road passes north of the forests in the east of the region. Thankfully, a network of 'B' and minor roads link all the off-road starting points for the cyclist, making the planning of longer tours, for a full weekend (or excessively fit individuals), simple. The Glen Esk public road runs into the heart of the region giving access to several routes, and the Cairn o' Mount road ties the region together from north to south.

Accommodation:— This area is not well provided for regarding accommodation. It is very much a working farming region with little provision for the visitor. Forest Enterprise seem almost alone in trying to attract visitors and accommodation is available only on the fringes, the main centres being Brechin, Montrose, Laurencekirk, Stonehaven and Banchory; all except Laurence-kirk having seasonal tourist information services. There are SYHA hostels only at Aberdeen and Glen Doll. Somewhat better provision is, however, available for camping and caravans. A sparse distribution of B.B's exists outwith main centres.

Geographical Features:— Angus (East) is a continuation of the mountain mass south of the River Dee. The area is crossed only by the 1500' Cairn o' Mount road (B974) and the Slug Road (A957). Glen Esk cuts deep into the region from the south. The high ground is, essentially, grouse moor - there is limited crag among the rounded outlines of the hills. Intensive farming surrounds the high ground, use being made of every bit of the fertile lowland soil. Afforestation has now clothed much of the former grouse moor to the far east of the region.

Mountains:- Mount Keen, the only Munro, is the highest and best known hill. It has a reputation for being very remote but is an easy day walk from Invermark, or a good half day with a bike, if fit. Use of a bike is the only sensible option from the north for the longer approach via Glen Tanar, especially since the demise of the bothy. It is a tedious hill to climb, but with exceptional views if clear. (Your author and his wife scaled its heights in thick mist - the bit about the view is based on study of maps and rumour!). The surrounding hills are rounded heather-clad humps of little individual interest, other than collectively creating a wild and remote landscape.

Rivers:- Much of the area is drained by the River North Esk which flows out into the North Sea via the beach in Montrose Bay. The Bervie Water flows out to Inverbervie and Cowie Water to Stonehaven. The northern forests drain into the Dee.

Forests:- The forests in the east all provide excellent mountainbiking, and some walking, though a bike is the only answer to a thorough exploration of the forests. Drumtochty, Doup of Becky, Fetteresso, and Durris all occupy the high ground and often reveal extensive views over the surrounding farmland. There is variety - each forest has its own character. It takes a week to cover them all!!

Lochs:- The sub-heading should be "Loch" as Loch Lee is the only sheet of water worthy of a mention here. It is natural and occupies a fine location at the head of Glen Esk.

Emergency:- All the lower glens are inhabited. Only the Mounth Road can be termed remote. Be careful not to get lost in the forests! Refer to the notes at the foot of page 17 which also apply.

Angus (East) Routes 1

Water of Saughs

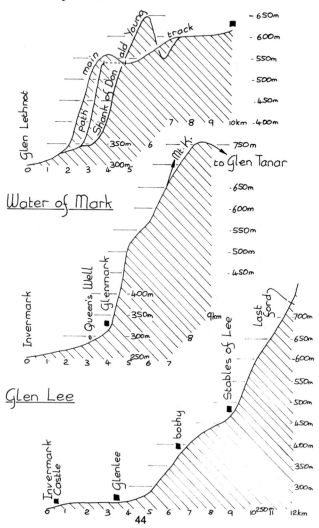

Water of Mark

Glen Lee

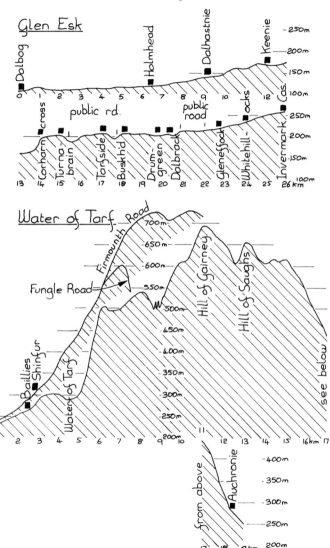

Glen Esk

Water of Tarf

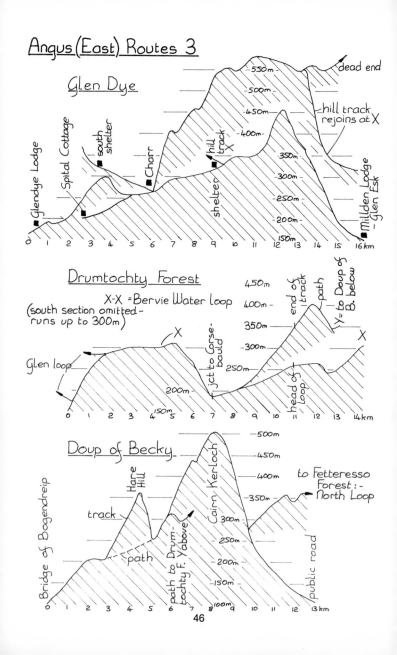

Angus (East) Routes 3

Glen Dye

- dead end
- 550m
- 500m
- hill track rejoins at X
- 450m
- 400m
- 350m
- 300m
- 250m
- 200m
- 150m

Glendye Lodge / Spital Cottage / south shelter / Charr / hill track X / shelter / Milden Lodge – Glen Esk

0 1 2 3 4 5 6 7 8 9 10 11 12 13 14 15 16km

Drumtochty Forest

X–X = Bervie Water loop

(south section omitted – runs up to 300m)

- 450m
- 400m
- 350m
- 300m
- 250m
- 200m
- 150m

Glen loop

X

jct to Corse-bauld

end of track / path / Y = to Doup of B. below

X

= head of loop

0 1 2 3 4 5 6 7 8 9 10 11 12 13 14km

Doup of Becky

- 500m
- 450m
- 400m
- 350m
- 300m
- 250m
- 200m
- 150m
- 100m

Bridge of Bogendreip

Hare Hill

track

path

path to Drumtochty F. Y above

Cairn Kerloch

to Fetteresso Forest :- North Loop

public road

0 1 2 3 4 5 6 7 8 9 10 11 12 13km

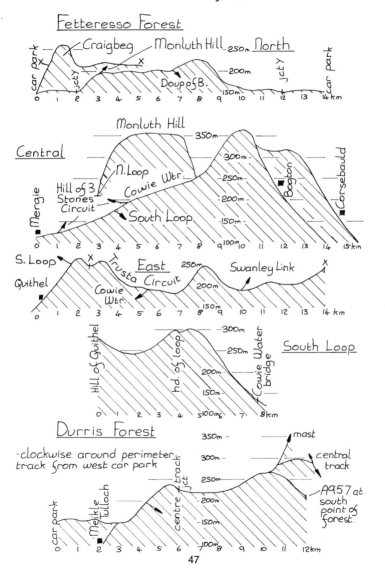

<u>Fetteresso Forest</u>

<u>North</u>
car park — Craigbeg — Monluth Hill 250m · jcty · car park · Doup of B. · 200m · 150m

0 1 2 3 4 5 6 7 8 9 10 11 12 13 14 km

<u>Central</u>
Monluth Hill — 350m · N. Loop · 300m · Bogton · 250m · Cowie Wtr · 200m · Corsebauld · Hill of 3 Stones Circuit · South Loop · 150m · Mergie · 100m

0 1 2 3 4 5 6 7 8 9 10 11 12 13 14 15 km

<u>East</u>
S. Loop — Trusta Circuit — 250m — Swanley Link · Quithel · Cowie Wtr · 200m · 150m

0 1 2 3 4 5 6 7 8 9 10 11 12 13 14 km

<u>South Loop</u>
Hill of Quithel · hd of loop · 300m · Cowie Water bridge · 250m · 200m · 150m · 100m

0 1 2 3 4 5 6 7 8 km

<u>Durris Forest</u>
-clockwise around perimeter track from west car park
350m — mast · 300m — central track · 250m · A957 at south point of forest · centre track jct · 200m · Meikle Tulloch · 150m · 100m · car park

0 1 2 3 4 5 6 7 8 9 10 11 12km

47

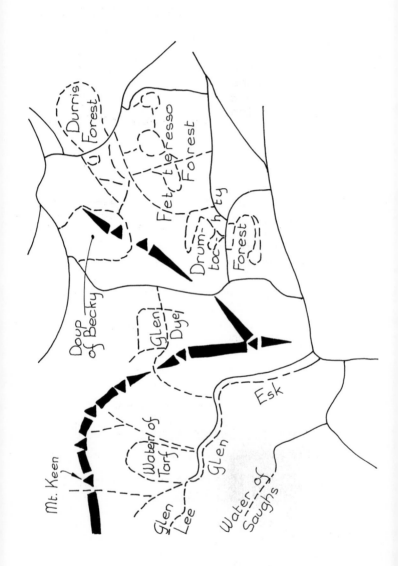

Durris Forest

Fletcheresso Forest

Drumtochty

Drumtochty Forest

Doup of Becky

Glen Dye

Esk

Water of Tarf

Glen

Glen Lee

Water of Saughs

Mt. Keen

48

The rough track following Water of Saughs starts from the end of the minor public road in Glen Lethnot (not named on the O.S. map). This minor road runs north west, then south west for some 11km or 7miles from Bridgend in Strathmore. The track, I repeat, is rough. Indeed, cyclists who cannot cope with steep stony tracks with deep ruts will not enjoy Water of Saughs. All is not lost however as a "circular" walk using the path over the Shank of Donald Young can be contrived. [Your author has to confess to not knowing Donald Young, and trusts his readers will share his guilt when walking over his shank!] The re-built Shieling of Saughs with its turf roof is a tribute to those who, having struggled to reach it, had the energy not only to re-build it, but to do so in such a sympathetic way. Congratulations are in order.   The distance from the end of the public road to this, the only shelter, is 10km or about 6miles whether or not Donald Young is disturbed.

<u>Shieling of Saughs</u>

Water of Saughs 2

Note:- the ford at 'X' may mean a return by the main track only.

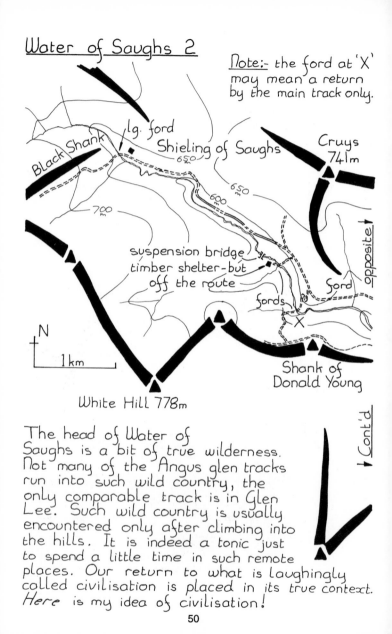

Black Shank

lg. ford

Shieling of Saughs

650

Cruys 741m

650 m

600 m

700 m

suspension bridge
timber shelter-but
off the route

fords

ford

opposite →

X

N

1 km

White Hill 778m

Shank of
Donald Young

Cont'd →

The head of Water of
Saughs is a bit of true wilderness.
Not many of the Angus glen tracks
run into such wild country, the
only comparable track is in Glen
Lee. Such wild country is usually
encountered only after climbing into
the hills. It is indeed a tonic just
to spend a little time in such remote
places. Our return to what is laughingly
called civilisation is placed in its true context.
Here is my idea of civilisation!

50

Walkers will prefer the zig-zag path 'X' (zig-zags not shown on the O.S. Landranger map), to the steep and very rough track at 'Y'.

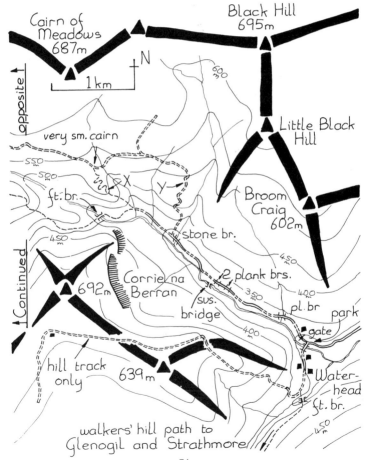

↑Continued Glen Tanar 6 ↑

Cairns and
boundary
stone

Mounth Road

Mount Keen
939m

800 m

700 m
750

eroded mess
with cairns

Y

cairns

Ladder Burn

600 m

550

524m

400

fords

fords

Glenmark

350

Queen's
Well

opposite→

X

N

1 km

path X continues-
becoming vague

Glen Lee

Hard
Hill

↓Continued

The Water of
Mark track soon
abandons the glen to
strike north past
Mount Keen. This
is the Mounth Rd.
The track in the
glen soon peters
out leaving Glen
Mark isolated,
in the middle
of nowhere.

52

Your author advises that point Y, opposite,
is the reasonable limit for a bike. The path
beyond is badly eroded, so please resist the
temptation to cycle the Mounth Road.
If you MUST this should
only be undertaken
in the driest
conditions, taking
great care not to
lock wheels or
skid or cause
ANY further
erosion to
this historic
route. Please
take note!!
Thank you.

Queen's Well

Note:- see Glen Esk
1 for detail
map.

Continued
Water of Tarf 2

preferred
route

park

Cairn

Invermark
Lodge

Continued opposite

Continued Glen Lee 3

Continued Glen Esk 2

Cas.

300 m

The head of
Glen Esk, right, is
very well connected
to adjacent routes.

53

Glen Lee 1

Glen Lee has everything. A pleasant lochside start followed by an open strath, then the track climbs to a high desolate glen. There is a fine waterfall to visit, a circular hill path to walk (opposite), even a castle! There is shelter if it rains. The complex start is explained in greater detail on page 58 (Glen Esk 1). Distances, one way, from the car park are:- Falls of Unich 6km (4 miles); the stable 9km (6 miles); and to the Last ford 11·5km (7·5 miles).

Stables of Lee

Muckle Cairn 732m (ish!)

650m

700m

Last ford

ford — 600m

ford 500m

Stables of Lee

761m

Water of Lee 550m

750m

Drumhilt 803m

Everan Hill 585m

805m

Easter Balloch 834m

N

1km

wire gate
plank bridge

Cont'd opp.

54

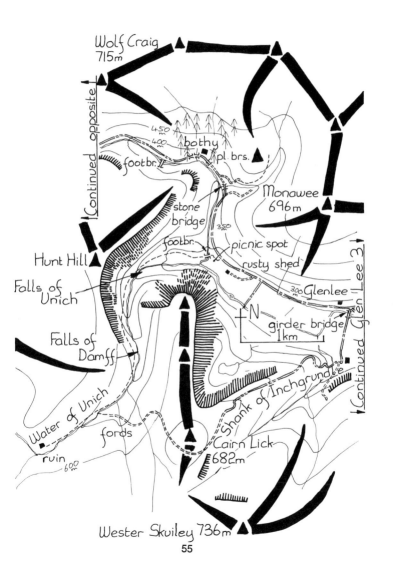

Wolf Craig 715m

Continued opposite

bothy

pl. brs.

footbr.

Monawee 696m

stone bridge

footbr.

picnic spot

rusty shed

Hunt Hill

Glenlee

Falls of Unich

N

girder bridge 1km

Continued Glen Lee 3

Falls of Damff

Shank of Inchgrundle

Water of Unich

fords

ruin

Cairn Lick 682m

Wester Skuiley 736m

Glen Lee 3

The bothy

Glen Lee 2

N

1 km

Continued Water of Mark 2

300 m

conc. br.

Castle

450
400 m
350 m
300

350 m

Loch Lee

Continued

300 m

450 m

Continued Glen Esk 2

Contd. Wtr. of Tarf 2

Note
For detail of the head of
Glen Esk refer to page
58 — Glen Esk 1.

Glen Lee 4

Invermark Castle

Glen Esk 1

The traverse of Glen Esk is possible on the 'wrong' side of the river, that is opposite the public road for almost its entire length. However, bikes are obliged to use the road for a short distance around Tarfside. Route finding is in places complex and your author has attempted to explain the difficult bits with detail maps. There is a pleasant stretch of riverside in the mid-section, an ideal lunch spot whichever way the route is taken. It is recommended to start at the head of the 22km or 14 mile route when cycling. An additional 4km or 2·5 miles extends the route to Edzell. Connections to the road are few, some are private or intrusive. Those of a nervous disposition will not enjoy the suspension bridges!! We start off with a detail map of the head of the route, also depicting the start of Glen Lee, Water of Mark, and one of the road connections for Water of Tarf:—

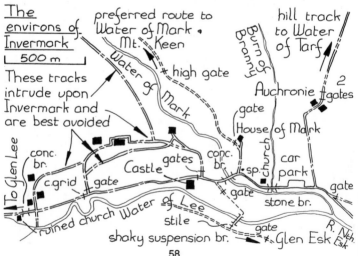

The environs of Invermark
|__ 500 m __|

These tracks intrude upon Invermark and are best avoided

preferred route to Water of Mark & Mt. Keen

hill track to Water of Tarf

Water of Mark

high gate

Burn of Branny

Auchronie 2 gates

gate

House of Mark

To Glen Lee

conc. br.

c.grid   gate

Castle   gates   conc. br.

church

car park

sp.

gate

gate

ruined church Water of Lee

stile

stone br.

gate

shaky suspension br. Glen Esk

R. Nth Esk

58

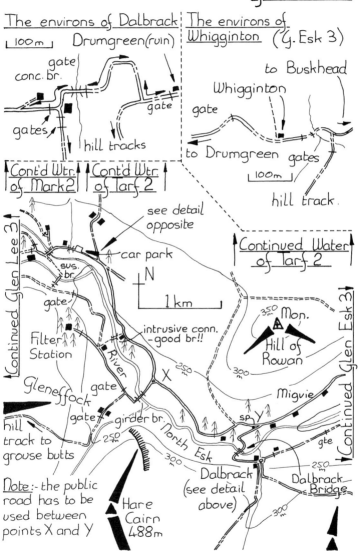

Glen Esk 3

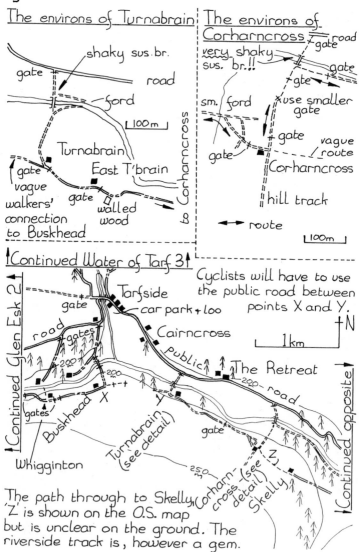

The environs of Turnabrain

shaky sus. br.

gate

road

ford

100 m

Turnabrain

East T'brain

gate

vague walkers' connection to Buskhead

gate

walled wood

to Corharncross

The environs of Corharncross

road

gate

very shaky sus. br.!!

gate

gte

use smaller gate

sm. ford

gate

vague route

gate

Corharncross

hill track

route

100m

↑Continued Water of Tarf 3↑

Tarfside

car park + loo

gate

Cairncross

Continued Glen Esk 2

road

gates

200

200

public

The Retreat

200 road

Cyclists will have to use the public road between points X and Y.

1 km

↑N

gates

Buskhead

X

Turnabrain (see detail)

Y

gate

Continued opposite

Whigginton

250 m

Corharn-cross (see detail)

Z

Skelly

The path through to Skelly, 'Z' is shown on the O.S. map but is unclear on the ground. The riverside track is, however a gem.

The environs of Keenie

The riverside track should be taken in preference to the track 'X' which peters out west of Skelly.

The environs of Dalhastnie

The connection to the public road via the Millden Lodge driveway is intrusive and not recommended by your author.

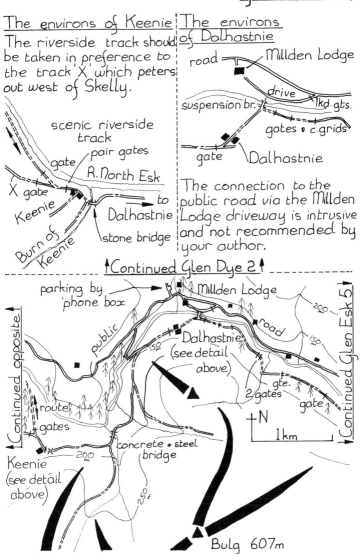

Glen Esk 5

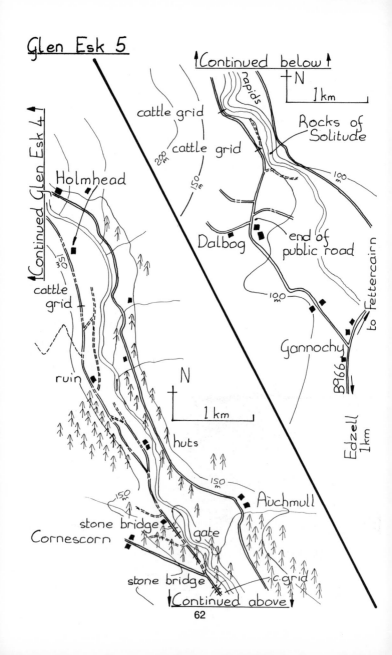

↑Continued below↑

N
1 km

rapids

Rocks of
Solitude

100

cattle grid

200m

cattle grid

150m

Continued Glen Esk 4↑

Holmhead

Dalbog

end of
public road

100

cattle grid

350m

ruin

N
1 km

huts

150m

Gannochy

B966

to Fettercairn

Edzell
1km

Auchmull

150m

stone bridge

Cornescorn

gate

stone bridge

c.grid

↓Continued above↓

Water of Tarf 1

The Water of Tarf track is out of bounds during the grouse shooting and deer stalking seasons. It neither all follows a glen, nor is it a right-of way. However the Firmounth Road and Fungle Road are rights-of-way, sharing their starting point, dividing, and both running out into Glen Tanar. These 'roads' are walkers' paths – the surface being unsuitable for wheels. The hill section of the track crosses wild moors and there is no shelter other than to huddle into a grouse butt! The loop totals 19km or 12miles, with the road connecting the ends of the loop adding a further 6km or 4miles. There is a car park at each end and even a loo at Tarfside (closed in winter - always a snag!)

Map Layout:-

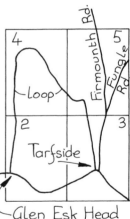

4

5

Firmounth Rd.

Fungle Rd.

Loop

2

3

Tarfside

Glen Esk Head

"That'll keep him quiet!!"
Your author congratulates the bridge builder on his sense of humour —on the condition the owner of the gloves and boots is not still wearing them!

Water of Tarf 2

↑ Continued Water of Tarf 4 ↑

N

1km

Hill of Kirny

Craig Brawlin 502m

cairn

600m

550m

500

450m

Corrie Duff

"loop" route

Badalair 536m

350m

Burnside

Badadarrach 525m

gate

300m

250m

462m

gate

gate

gates

Auchronie

Milton Cottage

← Contd Water of Mark 2

↓ Continued Glen Lee 3

Continued opposite →

gate

gate

Westbank

Hill of Rowan

Filter station

public

300m

gate

250m

road

Glen Effock

↓ Continued Glen Esk 2 ↓

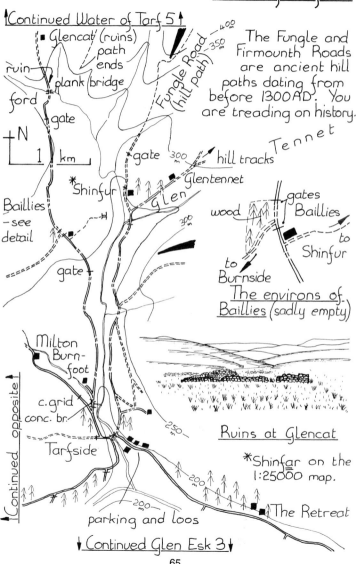

↑ Continued Water of Tarf 5 ↑

- Glencat (ruins)
  path ends
- ruin
- plank bridge
- ford
- gate

+N
1 km

The Fungle and
Firmounth Roads
are ancient hill
paths dating from
before 1300AD. You
are treading on history.

Fungle Road (hill path)
400
350

gate 300 hill tracks

Tennet

Shinfur
Glen Glentennet

300
m

Baillies
– see detail

gate

wood gates
Baillies
to Shinfur
to Burnside

The environs of Baillies (sadly empty)

Milton Burn-foot

c. grid conc. br.

Tarfside

250
m

Ruins at Glencat

*Shinfar on the 1:25000 map.

200
m

parking and loos

The Retreat

← Continued opposite ↑

↓ Continued Glen Esk 3 ↓

Water of Tarf 4

So near yet so far! The Water of Tarf track passes within only 600m of one of the hill tracks above Glen Tanar. See Glen Tanar 3 on page 114.

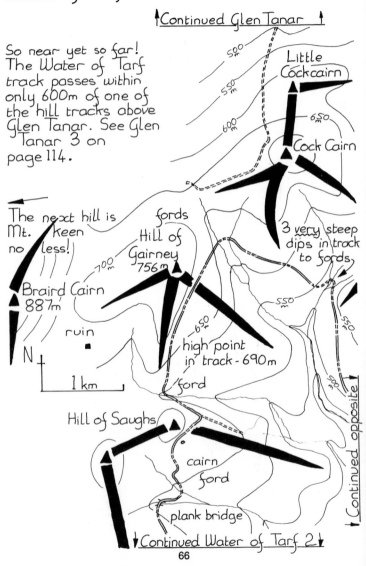

500 m
550 m
600 m
650 m

Little Cockcairn

Cock Cairn

The next hill is Mt. Keen no less!

fords

Hill of Gairney 756m

3 very steep dips in track to fords

700 m

Braird Cairn 887m

550 m

350 m

ruin

N

650 m

high point in track - 690m

1 km

ford

500 m

Hill of Saughs

cairn

ford

plank bridge

← Continued opposite →

↑<u>Continued Glen Tanar 4</u>↑

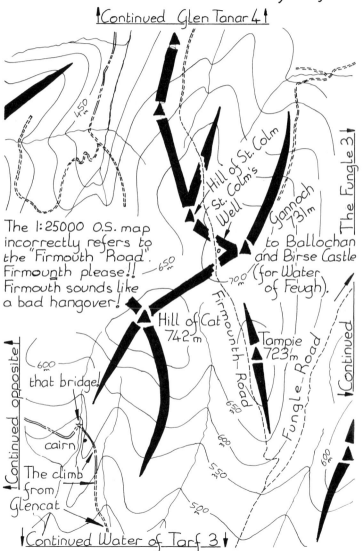

Hill of St. Colm

St. Colm's Well

Gannoch 731m

<u>The Fungle 3</u>↓

The 1:25000 O.S. map incorrectly refers to the "Firmouth Road". Firmounth please!! Firmouth sounds like a bad hangover!

to Ballochan and Birse Castle (for Water of Feugh).

650m

700m

Firmounth Road

Hill of Cat 742m

Tampie 723m

Fungle Road

↑<u>Continued</u>↓

600

that bridge!

cairn

The climb from Glencat

←<u>Continued opposite</u>↑

650m

600

550

500

↓↑<u>Continued Water of Tarf 3</u>↓↑

Glen Dye 1

Glen Dye runs west from the north side of the Cairn o' Mount road. [One of only two Mounth Roads to be improved to present day standards: the other is Cairnwell, the old Devil's Elbow pass.] I digress - back to Glen Dye! The track eventually runs into a hill path which continues to Millden Lo. in Glen Esk via the Burn of Turret. (The Burn of Turret is too short to be considered a separate route but a map showing the connection is included). There are two stone shelters and a bothy at Charr - not always open. A hill track loop runs to the north and roughly parallel with Glen Dye for those with surplus energy - but only outwith the shooting and stalking seasons. The route can be started from either Spital Cottage or Glendye Lodge. Distances are as below:—

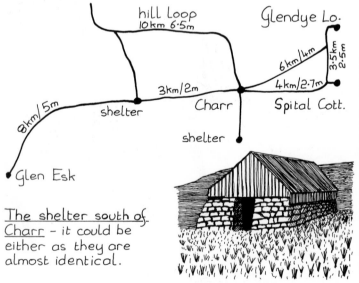

hill Loop
10km 6·5m

Glendye Lo.

3·5km 2·5m

6km/4m

4km/2·7m

3km/2m

Charr

Spital Cott.

8km/5m

shelter

shelter

Glen Esk

The shelter south of Charr - it could be either as they are almost identical.

68

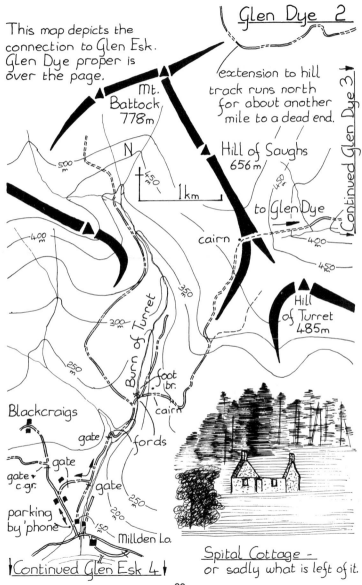

This map depicts the connection to Glen Esk. Glen Dye proper is over the page.

Glen Dye 2

extension to hill track runs north for about another mile to a dead end.

Mt. Battock 778m

Hill of Saughs 656m

N

500 m

450 m

1km

to Glen Dye

cairn

Continued Glen Dye 3

400 m

450 m

Hill of Turret 485m

350 m

Burn of Turret

300 m

250 m

foot br.

cairn

Blackcraigs

gate

fords

gate

gate c.gr.

gate

250 m

200 m

parking by 'phone

150 m

Millden Lo.

Continued Glen Esk 4

Spital Cottage - or sadly what is left of it.

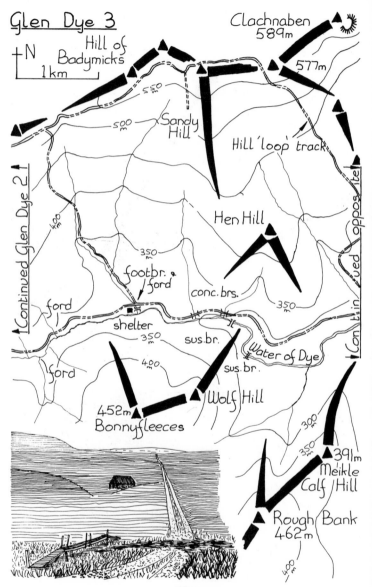

Glen Dye 3

N
1 km

Hill of
Badymicks

Clachnaben
589m

577m

550

500 m

Sandy
Hill

Hill 'loop' track

← Continued Glen Dye 2 !

400

Hen Hill

350 m

350 m

Continued opposite →

footbr. &
ford

ford

conc. brs.

shelter

350

sus. br.

Water of Dye

ford

400

sus. br.

452m
Bonnyfleeces

Wolf Hill

300

350

391m
Meikle
Calf Hill

Rough Bank
462m

400 m

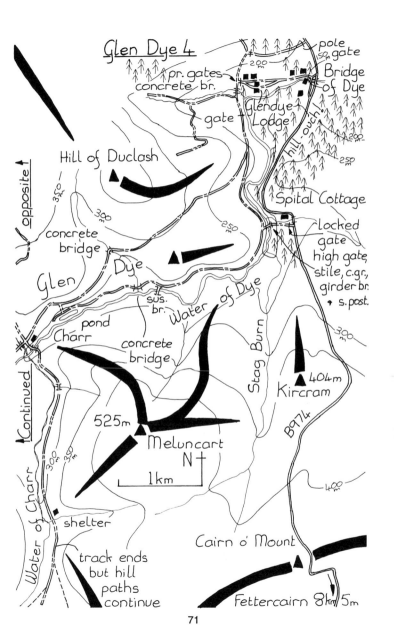

Glen Dye 4

pole gate
150m

Bridge of Dye

pr. gates
concrete br.

Glendye Lodge

gate

hill · och!

Hill of Duclash

Spital Cottage

concrete bridge

locked gate
high gate,
stile, c.gr,
girder br.
→ s.post.

Glen

Dye

Water of Dye

sus. br.

pond
Charr

concrete bridge

Stag Burn

Kircram

404m

opposite ↑

Continued ←

525m

Meluncart

N ⊤

1km

Water of Charr

shelter

track ends
but hill
paths
continue

Cairn o' Mount

Fettercairn 8km 5m

71

Drumtochty Forest 1

Drumtochty Forest centres around its main access point between Strath Finella and the Glen of Drumtochty. The forest provides both excellent walks local to the Glen and superb mountainbiking throughout. The forest is in three sections:—
1/ North (opposite) centred around the West Burn of Builg: this comprises both old and new tracks; a walkers' connection to Doup of Becky; a cyclists' connection to the vast Fetteresso Forest; and the track up Goyle hill. 2/ The central section (below), immediately north of the Glen of Drumtochty comprises a steep climb to a superb contour track ideal for walking or shorter bike rides, and the continuing connection north. 3/ The southern section (over the page), more correctly Drumelzie Wood, ideal for both walks and cycling, provides unrivalled views over Howe of the Mearns to the North Sea. Distances are to choice. There is no shelter, but there is a proper car park, picnic spot and loo at the start. The environs of Drumtochty Castle are private.

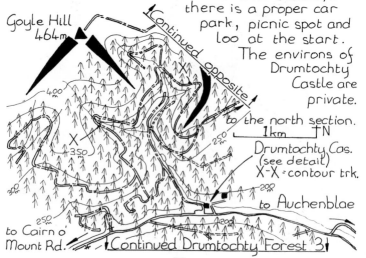

Goyle Hill
464m

400 m

X
350

300 m

250 m

to Cairn o'
Mount Rd.

Continued opposite

X

to the north section.
1km   ↑N
Drumtochty Cas.
(see detail)
X-X = contour trk.

250 m

200 m

to Auchenblae

Continued Drumtochty Forest 3

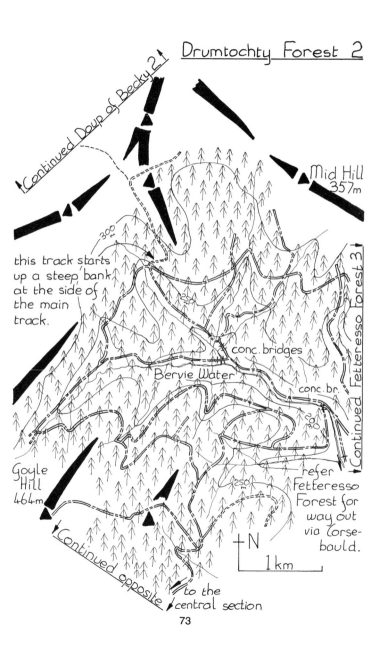

↑ Continued Doup of Becky 2 ↑

↑ Continued Doup of Becky 2 ↑

Mid Hill
357m

Continued Fetteresso Forest 3 ↑

this track starts
up a steep bank
at the side of
the main
track.

300 m

250

conc. bridges

Bervie Water

conc. br.

200

Goyle
Hill
464m

250

refer
Fetteresso
Forest for
way out
via Corse-
bauld.

↑N

1 km

↓ Continued opposite ↓

to the
central section

73

Drumtochty Forest 3

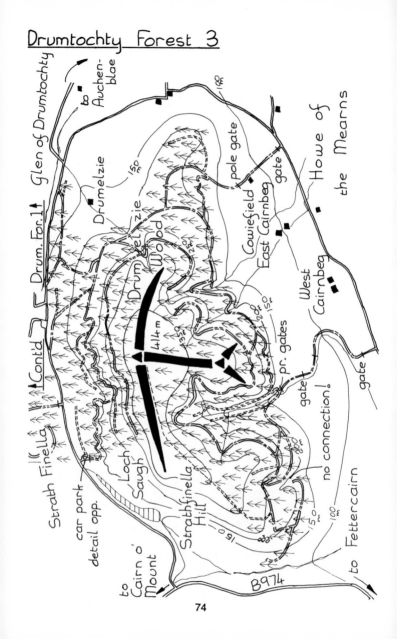

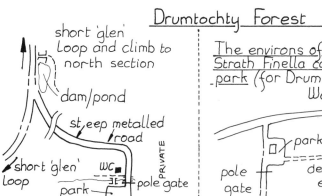

short 'glen' loop and climb to north section

dam/pond

steep metalled road

short 'glen' loop

WC

park

PRIVATE

pole gate

public road

The environs of Drumtochty Castle car park.

The environs of Strath Finella car park (for Drumelzie Wood).

park

pole gate

dead end

power lines

steep climb to contour track

Goyle Hill

Doup of Becky 1

The Doup of Becky tracks provide a hilly cycle ride based on Bridge of Bogendreip - a circuit of some 17·5 km or 11m, with some vicious gradients around the south west section. A walkers' path connects with Drumtochty Forest whilst good tracks continue into Fetteresso Forest and thence to Drumtochty Forest providing longer routes for bikes. Walkers may prefer to stay on the right-of-way shown opposite which bypasses the climb over Hare Hill. The 200m diversion to Kerloch at 534m is well worth it for the superb views.

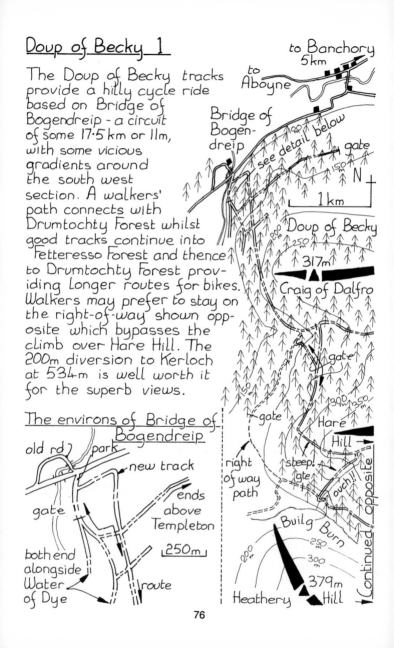

to Banchory 5km

to Aboyne

Bridge of Bogendreip

see detail below

gate

N

1 km

Doup of Becky

317m

Craig of Dalfro

gate

Hare Hill

steep!

gate

ouch!!

Continued opposite

Builg Burn

379m

Heathery Hill

right of way path

gate

The environs of Bridge of Bogendreip

old rd

park

new track

ends above Templeton

gate

250m

both end alongside Water of Dye

route

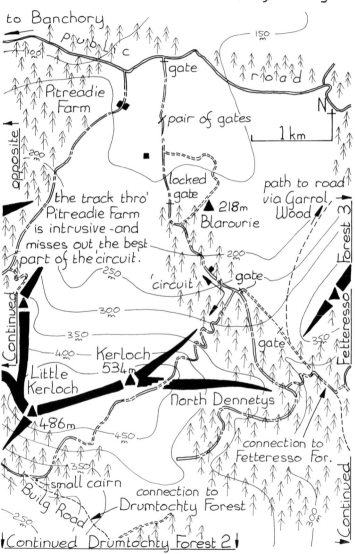

to Banchory

public

150 m

road

gate

Pitreadie Farm

pair of gates

N

1 km

opposite ↑

200 m

locked gate

path to road via Garrol Wood

the track thro' Pitreadie Farm is intrusive -and misses out the best part of the circuit.

▲ 218m Blarourie

200

gate

Fetteresso Forest 3

250

'circuit'

300

gate

350

350

400 Kerloch 534m

Little Kerloch

486m

North Dennetys

450

connection to Fetteresso For.

Continued

350

Builg Road

small cairn

connection to Drumtochty Forest

300

Continued

250

↓Continued Drumtochty Forest 2↓

77

Fetteresso Forest 1

Fetteresso Forest is mountainbiking country - mile upon mile of it! It does not, however, comprise endless tedious forest tracks. In a forest of such size there are always recently felled areas with views over the surrounding forest and beyond. There are three distinct sections:-
1/ The northern section (below and opposite). This is linked to Doup of Becky and (over Monluth Hill) the rest of Fetteresso Forest, starting from the A957 3 miles south of Crathes.
2/ The Cowie Water section with several road connections:- at Corsebauld, Bogton, Quithel, Elfhill and Mergie. All are linked by minor public road.
3/ The eastern section with a circuit around Hill of Swanley - again with connections to the same minor road.

Burn of Sheeoch

217m

concrete pipes/ford

Shillofad
368m

200

1 km

N

300

250

300

377m

conc. br./ford

350

300

Monluth Hill

Link to the Cowie Water (main) part of Fetteresso Forest

Doup of Becky 2↑

Continued opposite →

Cont'd

Cont'd   Fetteresso Forest 3↓

Distances in Fetteresso Forest are obviously to choice but at least *two to three days* are needed for a thorough exploration of the forest. As a rough guide the northern loop (left and below) is about 14 km or 8 miles from the car park at X. The Craigbeg loop is a mere 7 km or 4.5 miles from the same point, and the one-way distance from Corsebauld to Mergie is about 15 km or 10 miles.

There is, however no shelter anywhere in Fetteresso Forest – other than standing under one of the many trees!! Refer to the 'Link Routes', and the section on page 83 for planning longer tours in Fetteresso Forest and the adjacent Drumtochty Forest, Doup of Becky and Durris Forest. Even Blackhall Forest on Deeside, and Glen Dye, may be incorporated into longer tours from Stonehaven, Banchory and Fettercairn.

see detail below

Continued Durris Forest 1

X 200m

Continued opposite 1

250

300

Craigbeg

N

1 km

Continued

pole gates

mast

Cryne Corse Road

Cont'd Fetteresso For. 4

car pk. concealed from road

A957

SRWSoc. s.p.

pole gate

metalled road to mast

Detail at X

79

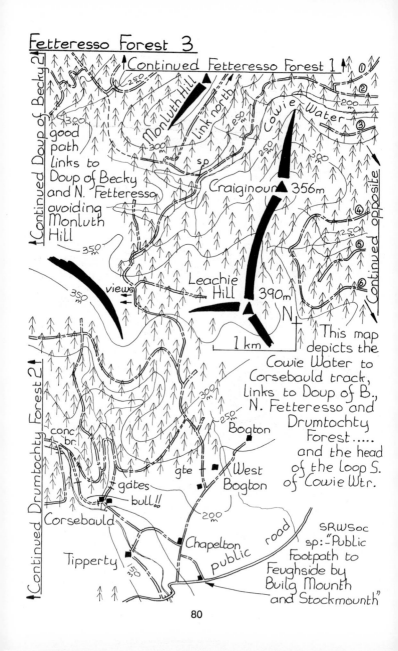

0

250

Monluth Hill ▲

Link north

250 m

Cowie Water

200

2

3

300

good path links to Doup of Becky and N. Fetteresso avoiding Monluth Hill

250 m

sp

300

Craiginour ▲ 356m

350 m

N.

4

250 m

5

350

views ←

Leachie Hill

390m

6

N ✝

1 km

This map depicts the Cowie Water to Corsebauld track, Links to Doup of B., N. Fetteresso and Drumtochty Forest..... and the head of the loop S. of Cowie Wtr.

↑ Continued Doup of Becky 2
↑ Continued opposite
↑ Continued Drumtochty Forest 2 ↑

300 m

250 m

Bogton

conc br.

gte

West Bogton

gates

bull !!

200 m

Corsebauld

Tipperty

150

Chapelton

public road

SRWSoc sp:- "Public Footpath to Feughside by Builg Mounth and Stockmounth"

80

↑Continued Fetteresso Forest 2↑

mast

300

public road

pole gate

Hill of
3 Stones
291m
pole gate

public roads

Mergie

250

Hill of
Hobseat
248m

conc.br.

150

lkd pole gate

conc. br.
pole gate

200

conc br

sp.

200

250

Hill of
Trusta
321m

300

Cryne Corse Road

Continued opposite

Continued Fetteresso Forest 5

250

250

pole gate

parking

N

gate

1 km

200

150

Quithel

public   road

① · ② connect
and continue
to Corsebauld
③ · ⑤ are dead ends
④ · ⑥ connect to
form 'south loop'

①②③ + ⑧ are
public roads.
④⑤ · ⑥ connect and continue
to Hill of Swanley.
⑦ runs out to Elfhill.

81

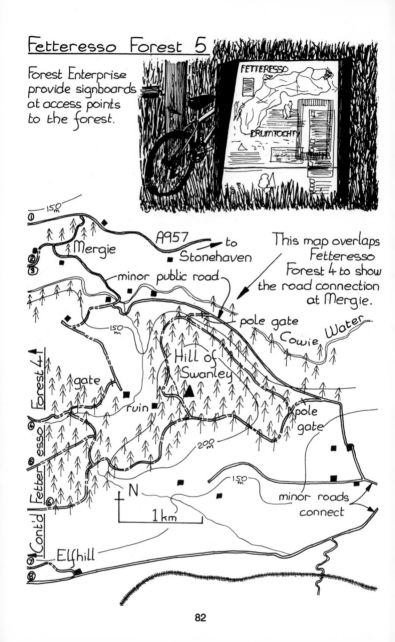

Fetteresso Forest 5

Forest Enterprise provide signboards at access points to the forest.

FETTERESSO

DRUMTOCHTY

150 m

A957 to Stonehaven

Mergie

minor public road

This map overlaps Fetteresso Forest 4 to show the road connection at Mergie.

pole gate

Cowie Water

150 m

Hill of Swanley

gate

ruin

pole gate

Cont'd Fetteresso Forest 4

200 m

150 m

N

1 km

minor roads connect

Elfhill

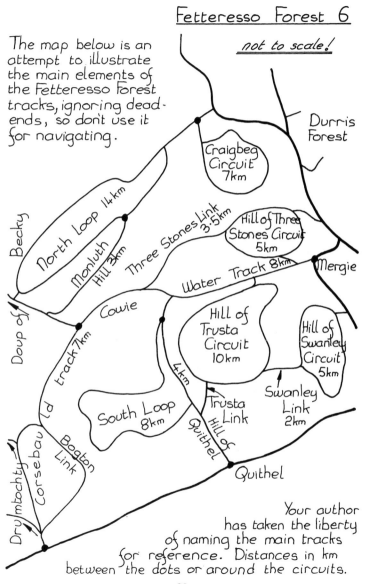

The map below is an attempt to illustrate the main elements of the Fetteresso Forest tracks, ignoring dead-ends, so don't use it for navigating.

not to scale!

Durris Forest

Craigbeg Circuit 7km

Becky

North Loop 14km

Monluth Hill 3km

Three Stones Link 3·5km

Hill of Three Stones Circuit 5km

Mergie

Water Track 8km

Doup of

Cowie

Old track 7km

Hill of Trusta Circuit 10km

Hill of Swanley Circuit 5km

Trusta Link

Swanley Link 2km

South Loop 8km

Hill of Quithel

4km

Corsebau

Bodbon Link

Drumtochty

Quithel

Your author has taken the liberty of naming the main tracks for reference. Distances in km between the dots or around the circuits.

Durris Forest 1

Durris Forest is the least interesting of the
region's forests but a half-day mountainbike
ride can be contrived from either the south-
west or the north-east sides of the wood,
both aspects having a couple of road
connections. A further connection
meets the minor road at the
northernmost extremity
of the wood. This minor
road conveniently links
all but one of the road
connections. A round
trip in Durris Forest
extends to about
13-16 km or
8-10 miles.

Meikle
Tulloch

park + pole gate

opposite

road

public

Gennel

100

150

200

Mundernal
324m

300

minor

lkd. pole
gate

car park

N

A957
1 km

lkd. pole gate

Cairn-mon-
earn

mast 378m

Cont'd

250

Continued Fetteresso Forest 2

lkd pair
gates

80

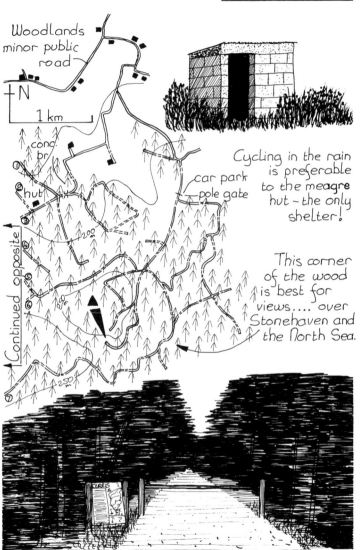

Woodlands minor public road

+N

1 km

conc. br

hut

car park
pole gate

200

Continued opposite

250

Cycling in the rain
is preferable
to the meagre
hut – the only
shelter!

This corner
of the wood
is best for
views.... over
Stonehaven and
the North Sea.

DURRIS

Deeside

Deeside

Access:- This area covers the south side of the Dee from just south of Braemar to Banchory. The A93 provides easy access, except of course if it is closed due to snow over Cairnwell, as it runs from Glen Shee right through to Aberdeen. From Balmoral to Banchory the B976 provides a quieter and less hurried access route, and indeed links together all routes but one - Glen Callater; a useful road for cyclists. To the east Cairn o' Mount, also regularly snowbound, provides another link south. Between the two present-day roads the ancient roads of the Capel Mounth, Jock's Road, the Firmounth Road and the Fungle Road provide walkers with access to Deeside from the south.

Accommodation:- Deeside is better provided for in terms of places to stay as compared with "Angus east" or "Angus west". A string of very pleasant villages all have good tourist facilities: Braemar, Ballater, Aboyne and Banchory all provide an excellent base. There is an SYHA youth hostel in Braemar, and caravan sites, camping and tourist info. at all the above. Braemar information centre is open all year. A good number of B.B's and hotels exist all along Deeside helped by demand from ski-ers.

Geographical Features:— The area is the 'north slope' of the great range of mountains extending from the Cairnwell to Cairn o' Mount roads. All water drains into the Dee. The area comprises remote hill country, moors, and the forests of Deeside. Well inland the winter cold is legendary (superb!)

Mountains:- Lochnagar is king (well, almost!) — "old man" and all! The high plateau region to the west gives way to more modest heights as one travels east, with the exception of Mount Keen. The spine of this mountain range is notable in that the southern Dee watershed rarely drops below 2000 feet until almost as far east as the Cairn o' Mount road.

Rivers:- Clunie Water, the River Muick and Water of Tanar are the three largest tributaries of the Dee, already a major river as it flows by Braemar - fed by the southern Cairngorms. The existence of the Mounth Roads means these tributaries are well provided with stone bridges (always an indication of the historic significance of a route), which, supplemented by more recent estate and forestry bridges, remove any problematic river crossings in the region.

Forests:- Trees, both 'natural' and for timber harvest are a major feature of Deeside, adding to its attraction rather than just blocking out the view. The Forest of Glen Tanar deserves a special mention as large areas of Scots pine are to be found (your author's favourite tree).

Lochs:- Despite its ice-age sculpted landforms this area appears to have less than its fair share of lochs. Loch Callater and Loch Muick are both entirely natural - no hydro dams here! The contrast between Loch Callater on a stormy day and Loch Muick in sunshine has to be seen to be fully appreciated. Dubh Loch, above Loch Muick is a small mountain loch in a magnificent location.

Emergency:- The remotest spot is probably the head of Glen Tanar. Your author makes no apology for repeating the point that the Mounth Roads are high mountain passes -and can be a serious undertaking in winter. The remainder of the routes are fairly tame, starting from populated areas. One eye on the weather is advised, especially in the upper glens and hills.

Deeside Routes 1

Glen Collater

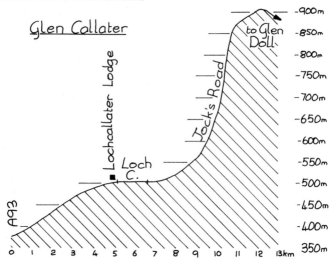

Glen Gelder

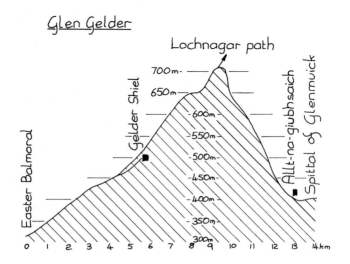

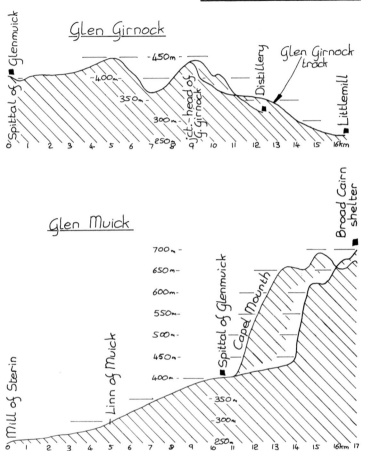

Glen Girnock

- 450m -
- 400m -
350m -
300m -
250m

°Spittal of Glenmuick

jct.- head of G.Girnock

Distillery

Glen Girnock track

Littlemill

0 1 2 3 4 5 6 7 8 9 10 11 12 13 14 15 16km

Glen Muick

700m -
650m -
600m -
550m -
500m -
450m -
400m -
350m
300m
250m

Mill of Sterin

Linn of Muick

Spittal of Glenmuick

Capel Mounth

Broad Cairn shelter

0 1 2 3 4 5 6 7 8 9 10 11 12 13 14 15 16km 17

91

Deeside Routes 3

Glen Tanar

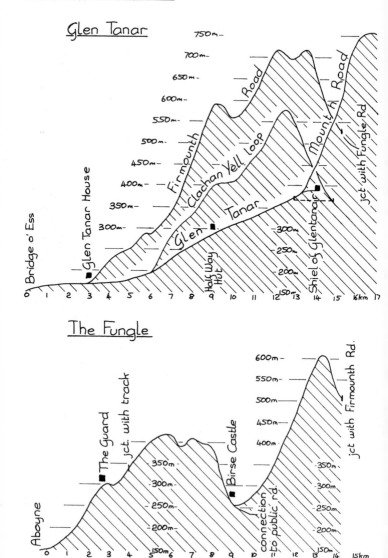

The Fungle

Ballater to Dinnet

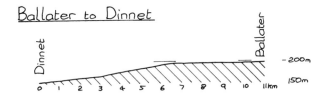

Blackhall Forest

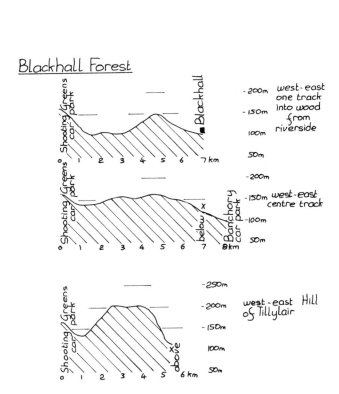

west-east
one track
into wood
from
riverside

west-east
centre track

west-east Hill
of Tillylair

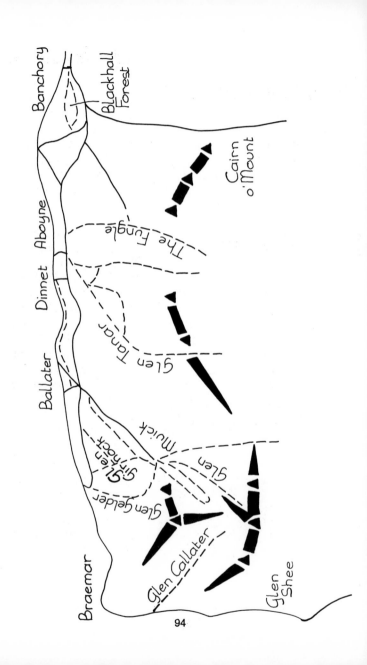

Banchory

Blackhall Forest

Aboyne

Dinnet

Cairn o'Mount

The Fungle

Ballater

Glen Tanar

Glen Muick

Glen Gairn

Glen Gelder

Glen Callater

Braemar

Glen Shee

Glen Callater 1

The Callater Burn drains into Glen Clunie (Clunie Water) before its waters reach the Dee. The glen has links with the Dee and, by Jock's Road, with Glen Doll. A good track extends to Lochcallater Lodge, from which a rough track continues along the south shore of Loch Callater, rejoining Jock's Road via a substantial ford. Jock's Road continues as a walkers' path to Glen Doll, the 5km (3 mile) upland section being a hill walk, necessitating the proper gear and navigating skills as it tops 3000 feet. The path is included as an important link between the glens. Further paths rise from Lochcallater Lodge - east to Lochnagar, south to Carn an Tuirc and west to Baddoch. There is a bothy - Callater Stables - by the Lodge, but it's a cold one!!

<u>Personal note:</u>- I owe Glen Callater an apology: In Book 1 I described the glen as "a dull, north facing glen....." This was based on two previous experiences in the glen, one wet bike ride abandoned in the rain, and the other a freezing cold, windswept walk from Glen Muick over Lochnagar one Easter, descending via Glen Callater to Braemar. Book 1 was to be THE BOOK. Little did I imagine that some years later I would be living in the Highlands writing Book 7! Research for Book 7, in Glen Callater, was undertaken one day in April 1996, with snow lying deep on the hills. The glen may have moods, but it is <u>never</u> dull; on a good day it may even be bright! I withdraw my insensitive use of the word "dull". I do hope Glen Callater will forgive me......   now get on with the rest of Book 7!

See page 96 for distances.

Glen Callater 2

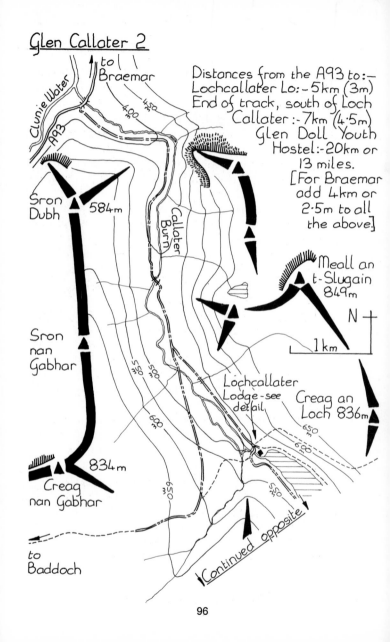

Distances from the A93 to:-
Lochcallater Lo:- 5km (3m)
End of track, south of Loch
Callater :- 7km (4.5m)
Glen Doll Youth
Hostel:- 20km or
13 miles.
[For Braemar
add 4km or
2.5m to all
the above]

to Braemar

Clunie Water

A93

Sron Dubh   584m

Callater Burn

Meall an t-Slugain 849m

N

1 km

Sron nan Gabhar

Lochcallater Lodge - see detail

Creag an Loch 836m

834m

Creag nan Gabhar

Continued opposite

to Baddoch

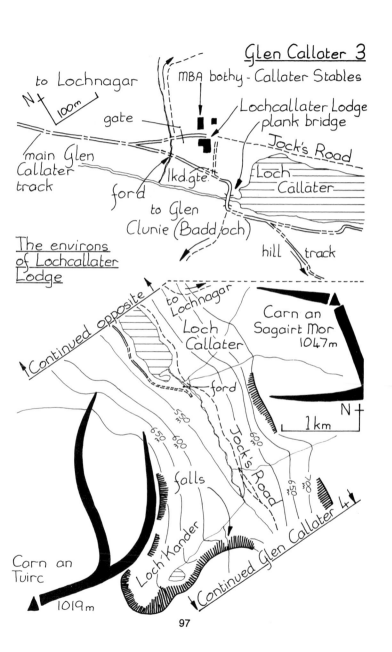

Glen Callater 3

MBA bothy - Callater Stables

Lochcallater Lodge
plank bridge

gate

to Lochnagar

100m

main Glen
Callater
track

lkd.gte.

ford

to Glen
Clunie (Baddjoch)

Jock's Road

Loch
Callater

hill track

The environs of Lochcallater Lodge

Continued opposite

to Lochnagar

Loch
Callater

ford

Carn an
Sagairt Mor
1047m

1 km

550
500
650
600
600
650
700
750
700

Jock's Road

falls

Loch Kander

Continued Glen Callater 4

Carn an
Tuirc

1019m

97

Glen Callater 4

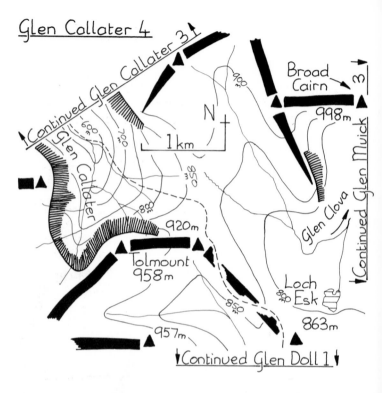

Continued Glen Callater 3 ↑

↑ Continued Glen Callater 3

Glen Callater

Broad Cairn
→ 3 ↑
998m

N

1 km

Continued Glen Muick ↓

Glen Clova

920m

Tolmount
958m

Loch Esk
863m

957m

850

↓ Continued Glen Doll 1 ↓

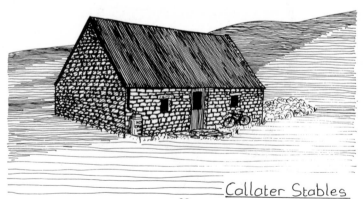

Callater Stables

Glen Gelder 1

This track runs from the Glen Muick car park to Balmoral on the River Dee. All is rideable but the Loch Muick end is rough, better in descent if cycling so start at Balmoral. The Balmoral end of the route appears intrusive but your author was reliably informed that the route depicted over is quite accessible to pedestrians *and* cyclists (thanks ma'am!). However yours truly bottled out of further exploration for fear of arrest! This route would make a good round trip if paired up with the right-of-way above Glen Girnock, except for the dubious (and pointless?) ban on cycles on the Glen Girnock (Abergeldie) estate. See page 102 for comment. The Glen Gelder route passes the 'tourist' path to Lochnagar and Gelder Shiel bothy, a favourite with climbers. The distance from Spittal of Glenmuick to Easter Balmoral is 14km or about 9 miles. There are fine views of Lochnagar en route.

The environs of Easter Balmoral

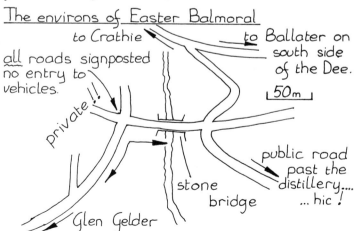

to Crathie

to Ballater on south side of the Dee.

all roads signposted
no entry to vehicles.

private!!

50m

public road past the distillery.... ... hic !

stone bridge

Glen Gelder

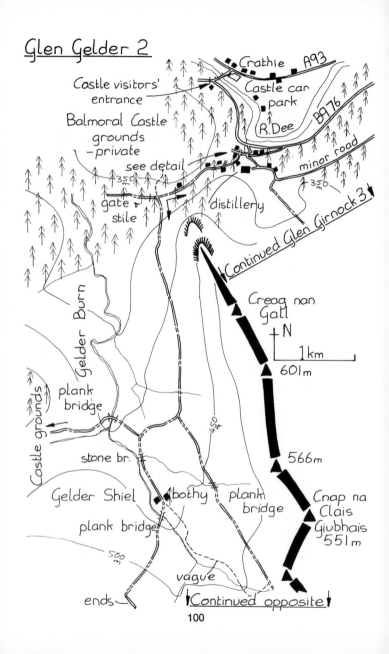

Glen Gelder 2

Crathie   A93

Castle visitors' entrance

Castle car park

Balmoral Castle grounds – private

B976

R. Dee

see detail

minor road

350

350

gate   stile

distillery

Continued Glen Girnock 3

Gelder Burn

Creag nan Gall

N

1 km

601m

Castle grounds

plank bridge

450

stone br.

566m

Gelder Shiel

bothy

plank bridge

Cnap na Clais Giubhais 551m

plank bridge

500

vague

ends

Continued opposite

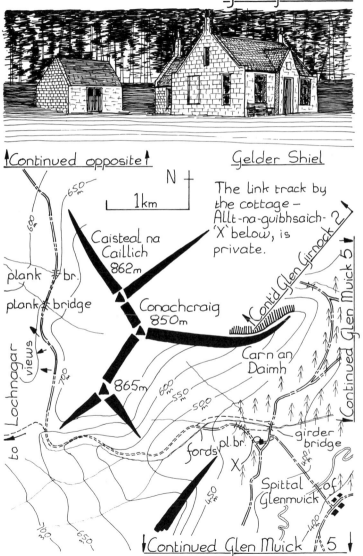

Gelder Shiel

↑Continued opposite↑

650 m

600

N +

1km

Caisteal na Caillich 862m

The link track by the cottage – Allt-na-guibhsaich – 'X' below, is private.

Cont'd Glen Girnock 2→

plank br.

plank bridge

Conachcraig 850m

←Continued Glen Muick 5→

Lochnagar views

700

Carn an Daimh

to ↑ Lochnagar

865m

600 m 550

500

girder bridge

fords pl. br.

X

Spittal of Glenmuick

450

400

700

650

↓Continued Glen Muick 5↓

Glen Girnock 1

The Glen Girnock tracks comprise a right-of-way from Easter Balmoral to Spittal of Glenmuick – a fine traverse on a good track – and a further track (not a right-of-way) down Glen Girnock proper. Abergelder Estate see fit to ban bikes from both sections – without apparent reason, no damage or nuisance could possibly be caused by a sensibly ridden bike on a hard-surfaced track. Your author's view is that this is grossly unfair, especially on the right-of-way section. In Glen Girnock proper a forest of timber has been used to construct a stile (more like a look-out tower!) more to obstruct cyclists than assist walkers. The signposts don't even say "please" let alone give a reason for such restrictions. We cyclists and walkers aren't daft, and are more likely to take note of reason than "No Bikes" – full stop. For those with a conscience this precludes the superb return trip from Spittal of Glenmuick or Easter Balmoral by Glen Girnock and Glen Gelder (which is not a right-of-way and permits the use of bikes!). Come on Mr. Landowner, be reasonable, and if you can't be reasonable, be polite ..... please. [Your author feels much better with that off his chest]. Meanwhile we just have to walk. Spittal of Glenmuick to Easter Balmoral is 12·5km (8 m); the Glen Girnock (proper) track runs 7 km (4·5 m) from the junction to Littlemill. There is an open shelter but we are probably not allowed to stand in it !!

Easter Balmoral — Littlemill

3·5 (2·25)

7 (4·5)

9 (5·75)

Spittal of Glenmuick

km (miles)

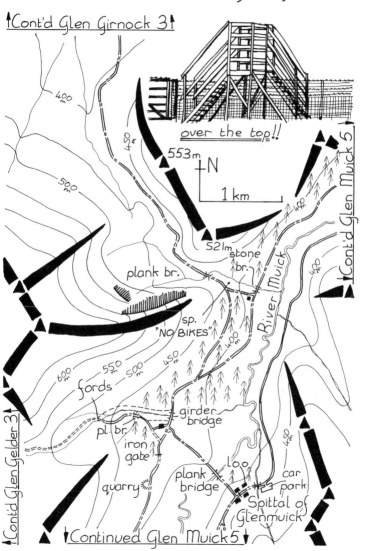

↑Cont'd Glen Girnock 3↑

over the top!!

553m

┼N

1 km

521m stone br.

↑Cont'd Glen Muick 5

plank br.

River Muick

sp. "NO BIKES"

400

600 550 500 450

fords

girder bridge

pl. br.

iron gate

quarry

plank bridge

loo

car park

Spittal of Glenmuick

↑Cont'd Glen Gelder 3↑

↓Continued Glen Muick 5↓

Glen Girnock 3

A further suggestion for the frustrated cyclist is to combine Glen Gelder and Glen Muick with the B976 to form a triangular ride of about 35km or 22miles, starting in Easter Balmoral, or approximately 39km or 24miles starting and finishing in Ballater. The 'B' road is reasonably quiet. This omits Glen Girnock.

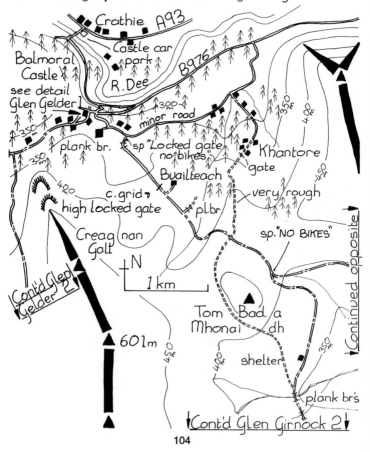

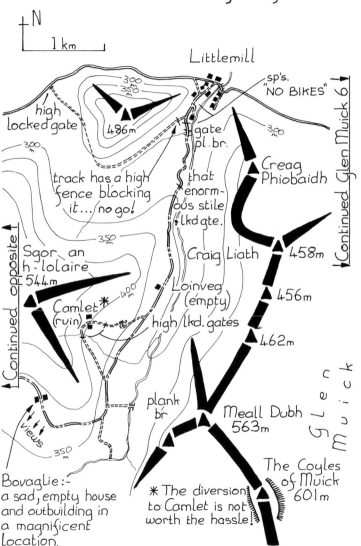

N
1 km

Littlemill

sp's. "NO BIKES"

300
350 m
486m

high locked gate

300 m

track has a high fence blocking it... no go!

gate
pl. br.

300 m

that "enormous" stile lkd gte.

Creag Phiobaidh

Craig Liath

458m

Continued Glen Muick 6

Sgor an h-Iolaire 544m

350 m

400 m

Camlet (ruin)

Loinveg (empty)

high lkd. gates

456m

462m

Continued opposite

plank br

Meall Dubh 563m

Glen Muick

views

350 m

The Coyles of Muick 601m

Bovaglie :-
a sad, empty house and outbuilding in a magnificent location.

* The diversion to Camlet is not worth the hassle!

Glen Muick 1

In considering cycling or walking in Glen Muick the immediate temptation is to drive to the car park at Spittal of Glenmuick. However cyclists especially would then miss the long, easy approach up a good track via the picturesque Linn of Muick. Cyclists are advised to start from Ballater. Once at Spittal of Glenmuick the options are numerous :- The Capel Mounth is cycleable as far as the top of the descent into Glen Clova (this steep descent should <u>not</u> be ridden or erosion would result); this is, of course, a fine walk. It is possible to walk or cycle to the shelter on Broad Cairn, from which walkers only may continue to its summit or follow the path down into Glen Clova. The circuit of Loch Muick is a popular walk and in places the path is rough; your author advises against the use of bikes on this. Glen Gelder makes an excellent bike ride or walk and passes the start of the Lochnagar "tourist" path. The traverse above Glen Girnock would be an excellent bike ride if a ban on their use were not imposed (see comment on page 102). Spittal of Glenmuick has a car park, loos, a mountain rescue post and a visitor/information centre. Distances are as set out below:-

Broad Cairn 2km (1.5m)

Glen Clova (car park) 8km (5m)

Easter Balmoral via Glen Girnock. (12.5km/8m)

Easter Balmoral via Glen Gelder 14km (9 m)

Loch circuit 11km (7.5m)

Spittal of Glenmuick

5km/3m

Mill of Sterin (start of easy track)

11km/7m

Ballater

Glen Clova car park via Capel Mounth 10km (6.5m)

8km (5m)

The environs of Spittal of Glenmuick

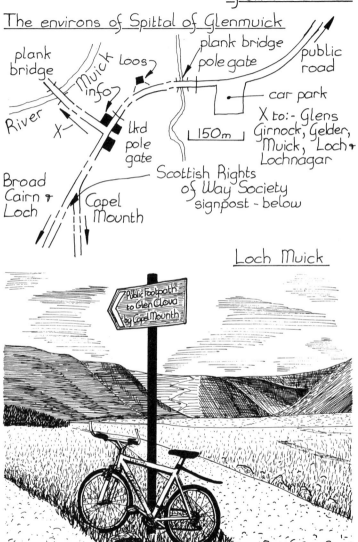

plank bridge

plank bridge
pole gate

public road

loos

Muick info

car park

plank bridge

River

X

lkd pole gate

X to:- Glens Girnock, Gelder, Muick, Loch & Lochnagar

150m

Broad Cairn & Loch

Capel Mounth

Scottish Rights of Way Society signpost - below

Loch Muick

Public Footpath to Glen Clova by Capel Mounth

Glen Muick 3

Path A - direct to Lochnagar.
Path B - to the Lochnagar 'tourist' path/Glen Gelder junction (indistinct).

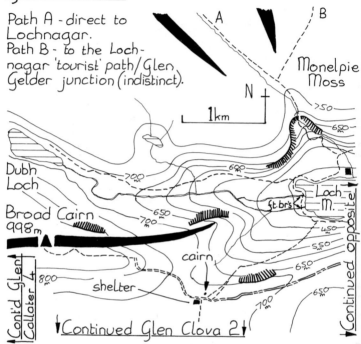

The Broad Cairn shelter

↑Continued Glen Muick 5↑

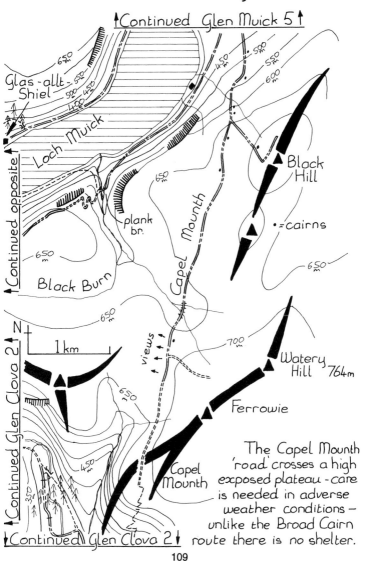

Glas-allt-Shiel

Loch Muick

←Continued opposite

Black Burn

plank br.

Capel Mounth

Black Hill

•=cairns

650m

N
1km

views

700m

Watery Hill 764m

Ferrowie

Capel Mounth

←Continued Glen Clova 2↑

↓Continued Glen Clova 2↓

The Capel Mounth 'road' crosses a high exposed plateau – care is needed in adverse weather conditions – unlike the Broad Cairn route there is no shelter.

Glen Muick 5

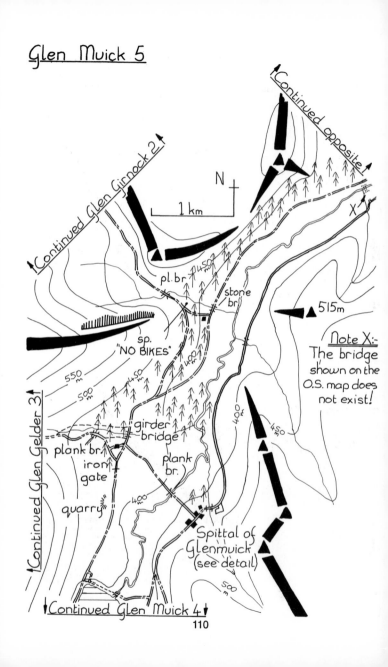

Continued opposite

Continued Glen Girnock 2

Continued Glen Gelder 3

N

1 km

pl. br.

stone br

▲ 515m

Note X:-
The bridge
shown on the
O.S. map does
not exist!

sp.
"NO BIKES"

550 m

500

450

400

450

girder bridge

plank br.

plank br.

iron gate

quarry

400

Spittal of
Glenmuick
(see detail)

500 m

Continued Glen Muick 4

110

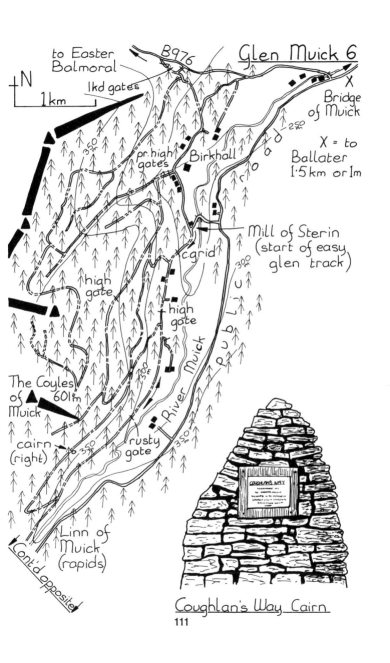

to Easter Balmoral

B976

Glen Muick 6

lkd gates

X
Bridge of Muick

X = to Ballater 1·5km or 1m

pr. high gates

Birkhall

Mill of Sterin (start of easy glen track)

c grid

350

250

300m

high gate

high gate

350

River Muick

PUBLIU

The Coyles of Muick ▲ 601m

cairn (right)

rusty gate

350

350

Linn of Muick (rapids)

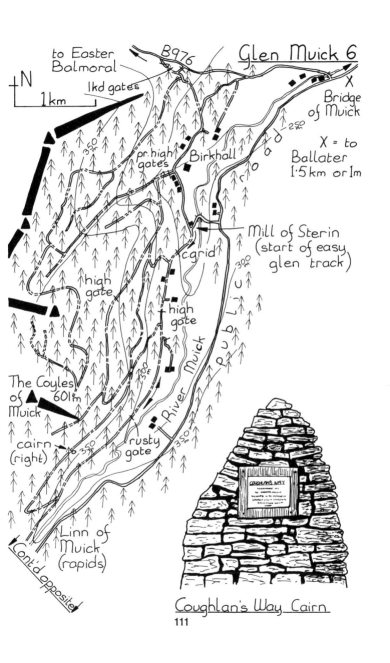

Cont'd opposite

Coughlan's Way Cairn

Glen Tanar 1

Glen Tanar is a gem. Starting off in picturesque Scots pine woods the track runs into the wild head of the glen, ending at Shiel of Glentanar, now sadly a ruin but up until recently a bothy- destroyed by fire. The Mounth Road rises from the glen head to pass over the west shoulder of Mount Keen before descending to Water of Mark and Invermark. South east of Glen Tanar a hill track encircles Clachan Yell - with a branch that almost meets the Water of Tarf track - see page 66. The Firmounth Road runs almost due south from Glen Tanar House and this ancient route can be explored either by the short loop around The Strone or, as a walk, all the way to Tarfside. It continues on Water of Tarf 5, page 67, where it is joined by the Fungle Road. The Fungle Road is dealt with separately in the next section but note several hill tracks linking the Deeside end of Firmounth and Fungle roads. A map showing the main tracks only with distances will assist route planning:-

Dinnet

Aboyne

5(3)   3.5(2.2)   3(2)

Br. of Ess

Glen Tanar House

3(2)

3(2)

The Strone

3(2)   Half-way Hut

5(3)

3(2)   Etnach

3(2)

3(2)

Shiel of Glen Tanar (6.5)   1(0.5)   1.5(1)

approx distances in km (m)

Clachan Yell

9 (6)

to Tarfside 14 km (9 m) -Firmounth Rd.

to Invermark 12 km (7.5m)-Mounth Road

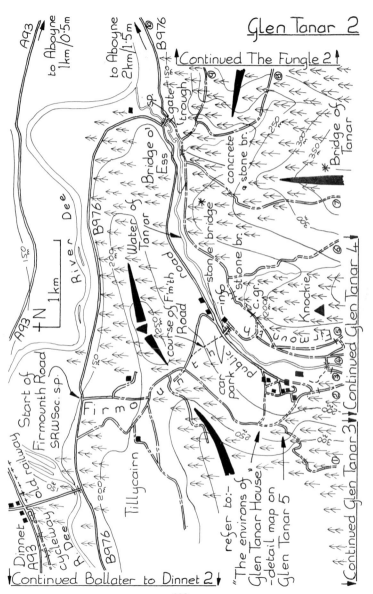

Glen Tanar 2

Continued The Fungle 2 ↑

Continued Glen Tanar 4 ↓

Continued Glen Tanar 3 ▼

Continued Ballater to Dinnet 2 ↓

A93
to Aboyne 1km / 0·5m

to Aboyne 2km / 1·5m

B976

Bridge of Tanar

Bridge of Ess

gate

trough

concrete & stone br.

stone bridge

stone br.

c.gr.

Knockie

Mount

Water of Tanar

B976

River Dee

A93

+N
1km

150

150
200

course of Firmounth Road

Firmounth Road

public car park

refer to:-
"The environs of Glen Tanar House"
-detail map on Glen Tanar 5

Start of Firmounth Road
SRWSoc. s.p.

old railway

cycleway R. Dee

Dinnet
A93

Tillycairn

Firmounth

B976

113

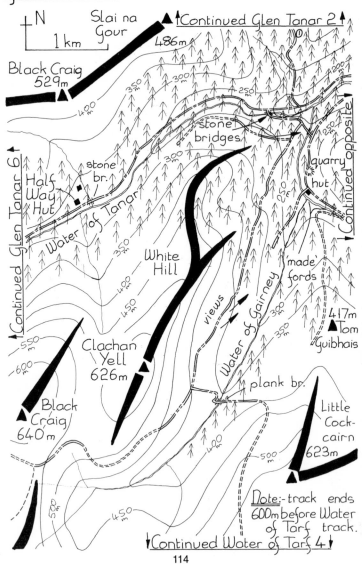

Glen Tanar 3

N
1 km

Slai na Gour

▲↑Continued Glen Tanar 2↑

486m

Black Craig
529m

350m
300m
250m
400m
200m

↑Continued Glen Tanar 6↑

stone bridges

stone br.

Half Way Hut

Water of Tanar

quarry hut

↓Continued opposite↓

300m

White Hill

'made' fords

views

Water of Gairney

417m
▲Tom Guibhais

350m

450m

Clachan Yell
626m

550m
600m

plank br.

Black Craig
640m

Little Cockcairn
623m

400m

500m

500m

450m

Note:- track ends 600m before Water of Tarf track.

↑Continued Water of Tarf 4↓

114

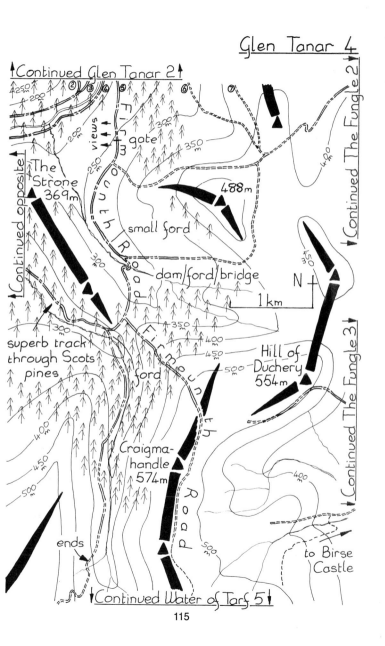

↑Continued Glen Tanar 2↑

↑Continued The Fungle 2↓

←Continued opposite←

250m
200
200
②③④⑤ ⑥ ⑦
250m

views → ←
gate
300

Firmouth Road
350m

The Strone 369m

488m

small ford

dam/ford/bridge

300

N

1 km

450m

←Continued The Fungle 3←

350m

Firmouth
400
450

superb track through Scots pines
300

ford
500

Hill of Duchery 554m

Craigma-handle 574m
Road
500m

400

ends

to Birse Castle

↓Continued Water of Tarf 5↓

The environs of Glen Tanar House

—preferred routes are indicated by arrows:—

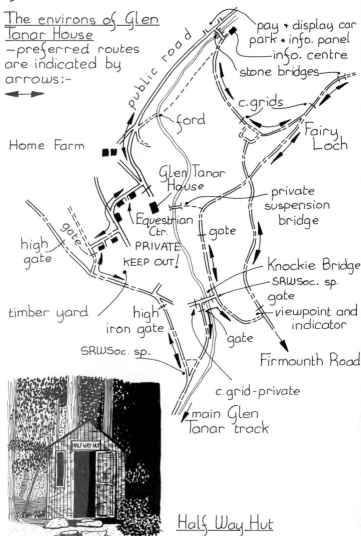

public road

pay + display car park + info. panel

info. centre

stone bridges

c. grids

ford

Fairy Loch

Home Farm

Glen Tanar House

private suspension bridge

Equestrian Ctr.
PRIVATE
KEEP OUT!

gate

high gate

gate

Knockie Bridge

SRWSoc. sp.

gate

viewpoint and indicator

timber yard

high iron gate

gate

SRWSoc. sp.

Firmounth Road

c. grid - private

main Glen Tanar track

HALFWAY HUT

Half Way Hut

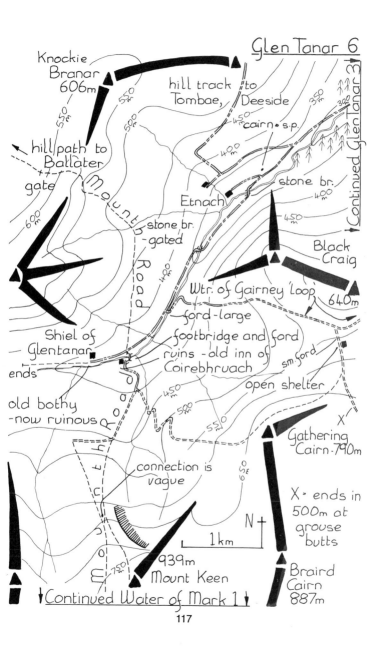

Knockie
Branar
606m

hill track to
Tombae, Deeside

cairn · s.p.

Continued Glen Tanar 3

hill path to
Ballater

gate

stone br.

Mounth Road

Etnach

stone br.
-gated

stone br.

Black
Craig

640m

Wtr. of Gairney 'loop

ford -large

Shiel of
Glentanar

ends

footbridge and ford

ruins - old inn of
Coirebhruach

open shelter

sm. ford

old bothy
-now ruinous

Mounth Road

connection is
vague

Gathering
Cairn · 790m

X - ends in
500m at
grouse
butts

N+

1 km

939m
Mount Keen

Continued Water of Mark 1

Braird
Cairn
887m

117

Glen Tanar 7

<u>The open shelter</u>
-by the Water of
Gairney "loop"

The Scottish Rights of Way
Society have provided many
signposts - especially useful
in the depths of the forest.
Well done lads!......
oops... and lassies!!

Public Right of Way
to Glen Esk by
the Mounth

To Ballater and
Glen Muick

To Dinnet and
Aboyne

<u>The bridge by Etnach</u>

The Fungle 1

The Fungle, after which the Fungle Road is named is a mini-glen just south of Aboyne. The track is steep to The Guard (a remote cottage) and continues as a path to join a hill track to Birse Castle. This section is hard going on a bike, first climbing, then rough, however the track to Birse Castle is good where a complex layout of paths and "non-paths" bypasses the private bits. Return by road is necessary for cyclists as the remainder of the Fungle Road, from Birse Castle to Tarfside in Glen Esk is too rough. The distance from Aboyne to Birse Castle/Ballochan is 10km (6.5 miles). Return to Aboyne by road is 20km or 13 miles. Continuing from Birse Castle/Ballochan to Tarfside is 13km or 8 miles. Careful study of "the environs of Birse Castle" is necessary to avoid getting lost, climbing fences, upsetting landowners etc. The track down to Newmill is also signposted as being out-of-bounds, illustrating the point that whilst rights of way are to be applauded, their existence tends to create a corridor with severe restrictions on each side. This has to be weighed against the possibility of blanket restrictions by landowners not sympathetic to the requirements of walkers and cyclists - and their need to get "away from it all". With a little tolerance there is surely space in the Highlands for us all.

o = SRWSoc signposts

Detail of the start
— from Aboyne

finding this bridge is the key to *not* ending up at the dead-end like your author.

to Craigendinnie

pl.br

stone gate posts

dead end

119

The Fungle 2

Cyclists face a big hill up to The Guard, a struggle to the signposts, and a good track only to the complex area around Birse Castle. Maybe it's far better to walk The Fungle!!

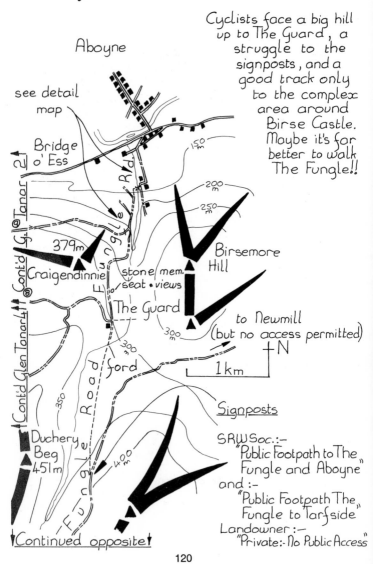

Aboyne

see detail map

Bridge o' Ess

Glen Tanar 21

(Cont'd Gl.' Tanar)

(Cont'd Glen Tanar 41)

Fungle Rd.

150 m
200 m
250 m
300 m
300
350
400

379m

Craigendinnie

stone mem. seat · views

The Guard

Birsemore Hill

to Newmill
(but no access permitted)

N

1 km

ford

Fungle Road

Duchery Beg 451m

Continued opposite

Signposts

SRWSoc.:-
   "Public Footpath to The Fungle and Aboyne"
and :-
   "Public Footpath The Fungle to Tarfside"
Landowner :-
   "Private:- No Public Access"

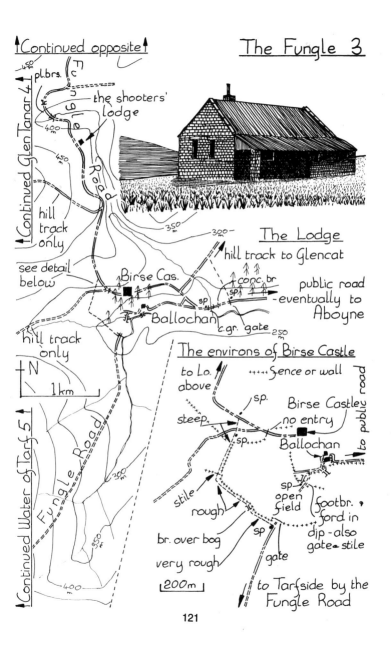

450
pl.brs.
Fungle
the shooters'
lodge
400 m

Continued Glen Tanar 4

450

hill
track
only

see detail
below

Birse Cas.

350m   300

The Lodge

hill track to Glencat

conc. br

public road
- eventually to
Aboyne

sp

Ballochan

sp

c.gr. gate   250m

hill track
only

N
1km

The environs of Birse Castle

++++ fence or wall

to Lo.
above

sp.

Birse Castle
no entry

steep

sp

Ballochan

Continued Water of Tarf 5

Fungle Road

300 m

sp

open
field

stile

rough

br. over bog

very rough

sp

gate

footbr. +
ford in
dip - also
gate + stile

to public road

to Tarfside by the
Fungle Road

200m

350 m

350

400

Ballater to Dinnet 1

The Ballater to Dinnet walkway and cycleway has been created on the old trackbed of the railway from Aberdeen to Ballater. This railway was intended to reach Braemar- with plans to pursue its construction via a junction at White Bridge (!) thence by Glen Tilt to Blair Atholl, and Glen Feshie to Strathspey -but that is another story. This simple route boasts a watering hole at each end; there is more point in the excursion if a start is made at Dinnet, as Ballater makes a better objective. The 22km or 14 mile return trip makes an excellent evening excursion on a bike, and a midge-beating speed can easily be maintained in both directions! An easy half-day walk can cover the route in one direction.

+N

1km

B972

plank br.

seats

or seat

picnic table

A93

R. Dee

old station

B976

Ballater

250
m

A93

A93

pl. br's.

ramps to busy road crossing -care!

200
m

250
m

A93

250
m

200
m

250
m

Continued "opposite"

'sleepers' are added to the usual grading when the route is on the old railway :-

Let's hope the walkway will one day be extended to Aboyne. A lump of infrastructure like this should not be wasted.

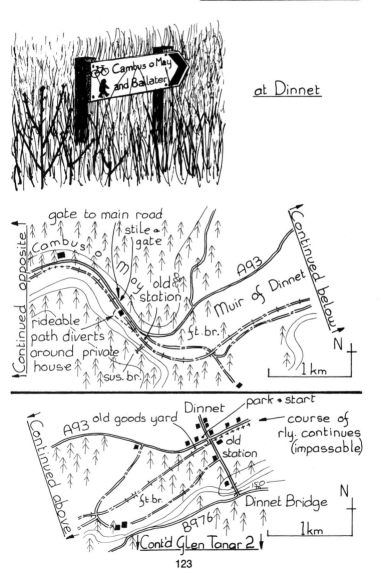

at Dinnet

gate to main road

stile gate

Cambus o May

old station

A93

Muir of Dinnet

Continued opposite

Continued below

rideable path diverts around private house

ft. br.

sus. br.

N

1 km

Dinnet   park • start

A93   old goods yard

← course of rly. continues (impassable)

old station

Continued above

ft. br.

150

Dinnet Bridge

B976

N

1km

Cont'd Glen Tanar 2 ↓

Blackhall Forest 1

Blackhall Forest, otherwise known as Banchory Forest, does not, from a cursory glance at the O.S. map, appear to have much potential for walkers and cyclists. However, this elevated woodland on the banks of the Dee boasts not only picturesque riverside trails but viewpoints overlooking the surrounding countryside. Walks start from either of the two car parks, Shooting Greens, or the new one for Scolty, whilst cyclists can spend all day happily tiring themselves out on the many alternative grades of path and track. Just one note of caution: the footpaths do get busy at weekends and holiday times, so cyclists are better keeping to the main forest tracks at these times. Distance is to choice.

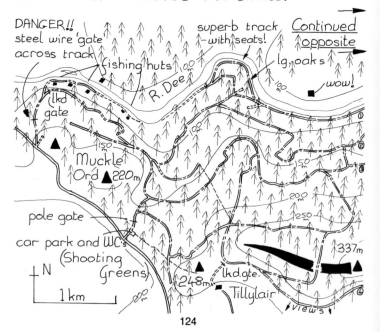

DANGER!!
steel wire 'gate
across track

fishing huts

superb track
—with seats!

Continued opposite

lg oaks

wow!

lkd gate

R. Dee

100

100

100

Muckle Ord ▲220m

150

150

200

250m

pole gate

car park and WC's
(Shooting Greens)

N

1 km

248m

lkd. gte.

Tillylair

views

337m

124

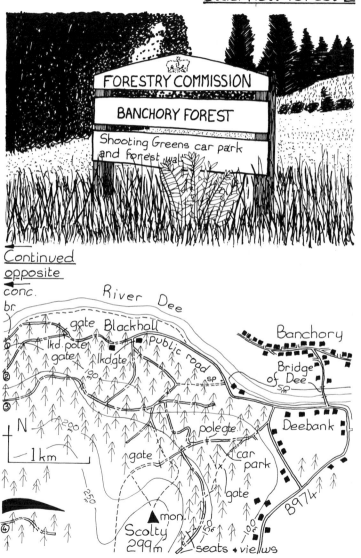

FORESTRY COMMISSION

BANCHORY FOREST

Shooting Greens car park
and forest walk

Continued
opposite
←

conc.
br.

River Dee

gate Blackhall
lkd pole
gate lkdgte
100
public road
sp

Banchory

Bridge
of Dee
sp

N
1km
200
250

polegte
gate
car
park

gate

250
mon.
Scolty
299m
seats ♦ views

Deebank

B974

125

Link Routes

The link routes shown demonstrate how long through routes are made up from the various page maps. Variations can be planned using further adjacent routes but these should provide a basis for extended exploration.

The West Angus Glens   Link Route 1

The west Angus glens are nearly all linked by paths - and tied into Glen Callater by Jock's Road. The Glen Clova to Broad Cairn track link to Glen Muick (see link route 5) also ties in. These give the opportunity for many a long-distance walk of several days duration, though apart from Glen Doll Youth Hostel, camping is the only practical overnight option. Suggested walks are from Glen Isla to Glen Muick and beyond, or from Backwater Reservoir to Braemar. These routes are <u>not</u> suitable for cyclists.

Backwater to Braemar

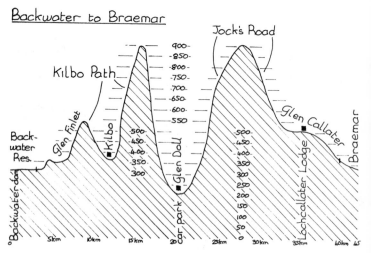

126

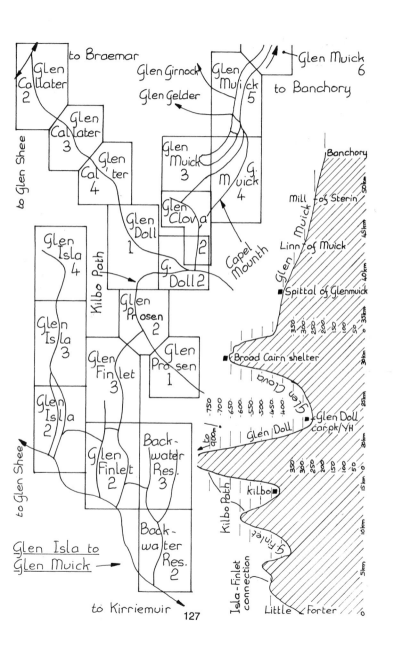

to Braemar

Glen Callater 2

Glen Callater 3

Glen Cal,ter 4

to Glen Shee

Glen Girnock

Glen Muick 5

Glen Muick 6

to Banchory

Glen Gelder

Glen Muick 3

G. Muick 4

Glen Doll 1

Glen Clova 2

Capel Mount

G. Doll 2

Kilbo Path

Glen Isla 4

Glen Prosen 2

Glen Isla 3

Glen Finlet 3

Glen Prosen 1

Glen Isla 2

to Glen Shee

Glen Finlet 2

Back-water Res. 3

Glen Isla to Glen Muick →

Back-water Res. 2

to Kirriemuir 127

Banchory

Mill of Sterin

Glen Muick

Linn of Muick

Spittal of Glenmuick

350 300 250 200 150 100 50 0 km

50 km

45 km

40 km

35 km

Broad Cairn shelter

30 km

Glen Clova

-750 -700 -650 -600 -550 -500 -450 -400

to 900 m

Glen Doll

Glen Doll car pk/YH

350 300 250 200 150 100 50 0 km

25 km

20 km

Kilbo Path

kilbo

15 km

G. Finlet

Isla-Finlet connection

Little Forter

10 km

5 km

0

Edzell to Aboyne

A superb through route almost entirely off-road, although the central section around Mount Keen should not be cycled due to severe erosion problems.

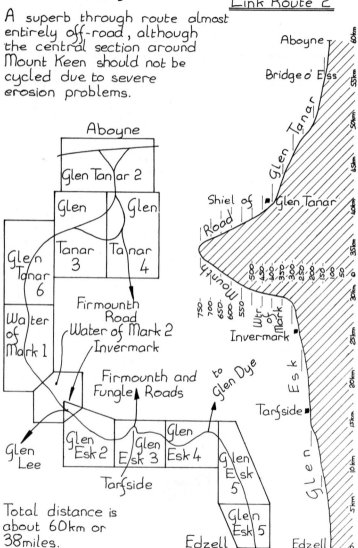

Total distance is about 60km or 38 miles.

128

The Fungle and Firmounth

Link Route 3

Two shorter alternatives to the route depicted opposite, sharing both start and finishing points. A feasible circular walk using routes 2,3, but not suitable as an off-road cycle route.
Both routes 2+3 cover high ground and a sharp eye should be kept on the weather.

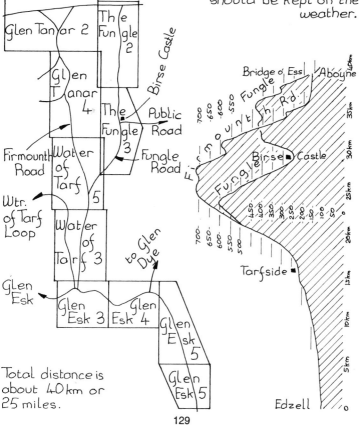

Glen Tanar 2

The Fungle 2

Birse Castle

Glen Tanar 4

The Fungle 3

Public Road

Firmounth Road

Water of Tarf 5

Fungle Road

Wtr. of Tarf Loop

Water of Tarf 3

to Glen Dye

Glen Esk

Glen Esk 3

Glen Esk 4

Glen Esk 5

Glen Esk 5

Total distance is about 40 km or 25 miles.

Bridge o' Ess Aboyne
Fungle th Rd
Firmounth
Fungle
Birse Castle
Tarfside
Edzell

40km
35km
30km
25km
20km
15km
10km
5km
0

700 650 600 550
450 400 350 300 250 100 50
700 650 600 550 500

The Eastern Forests

At last - a 'link route' for cyclists!
The combination of Drumtochty Forest, Fetteresso Forest, Durris Forest and Doup of Becky provide the cyclist with a variety of through routes, especially if also using the surrounding minor roads to assist a return to base. In contrast to the preceding 'link routes' this area is not particularly suited to the walker - much better possibilities for long walks lie to the west. However, this is a mountainbikers' paradise! No gradient profile is shown here as the possibilities are endless. It is worth spending a few minutes studying the O.S. map, this book (of course!) and

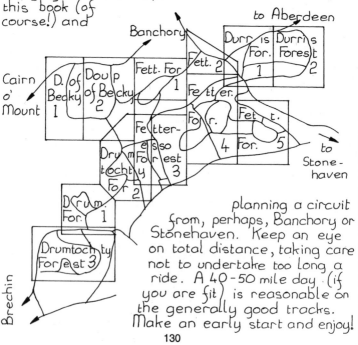

planning a circuit from, perhaps, Banchory or Stonehaven. Keep an eye on total distance, taking care not to undertake too long a ride. A 40-50 mile day (if you are fit) is reasonable on the generally good tracks. Make an early start and enjoy!

130

Dinnet to Balmoral

Link Route 5

A 40km/25 mile route forming an ideal day out on a mountainbike. Returning by the B976 adds a further 24km or 15 miles. The return by road is mostly downhill, and with the prevailing wind behind, the best direction for this circuit is as described.

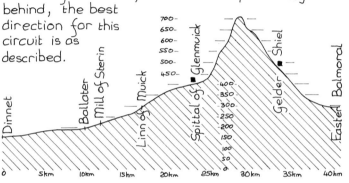

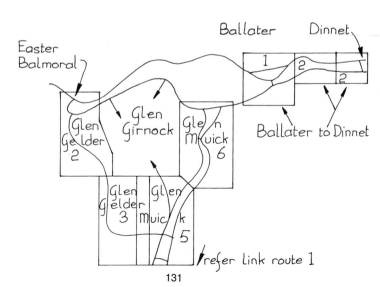

The Mounth Roads

Although not fitting comfortably into the 'glen' theme of this series of guidebooks it would be a grave omission to make only passing reference to the Mounth Roads. Dating from the thirteenth century, or even earlier, these were once the main trading (and thieving!) routes in the area. The steep hill routes were no obstacle (in summer) as wheeled transport was virtually unusable until the mid eighteenth century and the introduction of made up turnpike roads – and this was only one-hundred-odd years before the region saw the first railways. Anyway, this is not a history book but a guide to the glens! A brief description of each of these roads is given; as the tracing of these routes deserves separate study, details of maps and further reading are given. A "thumb nail" map gives the location of each "road". I assume you already have the OS 1:50000 series Landranger maps but serious interest in tracing these routes will be rewarded by close study of the 1:25000 series of appropriately named Pathfinder maps. Further recommended reading is as follows:-
"Scottish Hill Tracks" published by the Scottish Rights of Way Society ISBN 0-950281 158.
"Grampian Ways" by Robert Smith - a fascinating history of the Roads ISBN 1-870978 404.
"The Drove Roads of Scotland" by A.R.B. Haldane - a detailed text-book on the Drovers 'industry' in Scotland ISBN 1-874744 769.
<u>Note ①</u> Distances in the following pages are given in km/m between the circled points.
<u>Note ②</u> All the Mounth Roads are walks, rather than cycle rides due to rough terrain and existing and potential erosion problems. Please take great care of our history! Obviously, the

Cairnwell and Cairn o' Mount, now public roads, can be ridden.

<u>Note ③</u> The following routes are by no means an exhaustive list (exhausting, maybe!), but representing the 'A' roads of long ago. There existed a network of connections and short cuts – especially on the lower ground – and of course, a national network of drove roads existed. Later, that is after 1745, military roads and then the turnpike roads allowed the use of wheeled traffic. It is perhaps ironic that your author now has to advise against the use of cycles on the high passes due to possible erosion problems. What, one wonders, were the erosion problems in the days of cattle droving?

The White Mounth

Probably used as a drovers' short cut from Braemar to Spittal of Glenmuick before crossing the Capel Mounth to Glen Clova. This, the highest of the passes is a serious mountain walk, especially in winter conditions.

Landranger Nos:- 43, 44.

Pathfinder Nos:- 255, 269, 270.

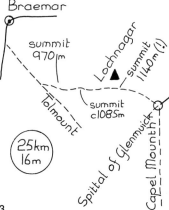

Note! Much of the route is over 900m/3000ft.

Braemar

summit 970m

Lochnagar

summit 1140m (!)

Tolmount

summit c1085m

25km 16m

Capel Mounth

Spittal of Glenmuick

133

The Cairnwell Pass

One of only two Mounth Roads to become a public road. Once boasting the notorious 'Devil's Elbow' hairpin bend - now straightened out but still visible by the roadside. The summit is spoilt by car parks and all the paraphernalia associated with ski-ing. Despite this mass tourism Braemar retains its dignity.

Landranger No:- 43.

Pathfinder Nos:- 269, 282, 295.

The Monega Pass

Once an alternative to the Cairnwell and seeking even higher (and drier) ground, the Monega Pass runs from Glen Clunie to Glen Isla. Barely traceable at its northern end but a good track as it descends into Glen Isla

Landranger No:- 43.

Pathfinder Nos:- 269, 282.

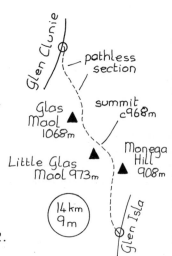

The Tolmount (Jock's Road)

Running from Braemar (Glen Callater) to Glen Doll, the Tolmounth, also known as Jock's Road covers a considerable length of very high ground and is a committing walk. It is a footpath from Glencallater Lodge until just above Glen Doll Youth Hostel. The high section can be difficult to follow.

Landranger Nos:- 43, 44.

Pathfinder Nos:- 269, 270, 283

Braemar

Glen Clunie

■ Glencallater Lodge

Crow Craigies 920m

summit c 908m

Glen Doll

Glen Clova

Kilbo Path

(24km 15m)

The Kilbo Path

A cross-country path from Kirkton of Glenisla via Glen Finlet to Glen Doll, dipping to the ruin, Kilbo at its mid-point, at the head of Glen Prosen. Care is needed navigating the upper section especially if heading for Glen Doll in mist.

Landranger No:- 44.

Pathfinder Nos:- 283, 296.

Glen Doll

Glen Clova

summit c 835m

♦ Kilbo

Glen Prosen

summit 586m

Glen Finlet

(22km 14m)

Kirkton of Glenisla

The Capel Mounth

This route runs from Ballater to
Glen Clova, encompassing most
of Glen Muick. A high level
track then runs south and
drops steeply (as a path,
precluding the use of
cycles) into Glen Clova.
Named as the "Capel
Road" on the O.S.
Pathfinder map.

Landranger No:- 44.

Pathfinder Nos:- 256,
            270, 283.

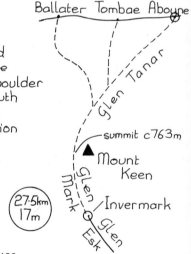

The Mounth Road

A once-important route
from Ballater, Tombae
and Aboyne via the head
of Glen Tanar (complete
with its inn), over the shoulder
of Mount Keen and south
to Glen Mark and Glen
Esk. Only a short section
is on a footpath, the
remainder is on tracks.

Landranger No:- 44.

Pathfinder Nos:- 256,
            257, 271.

The Firmounth Road

Also known as the Fir Mounth (two words) or Mounth Gammel, this route extends from Dinnet on Deeside, crossing Glen Tanar and proceeding to Tarfside in Glen Esk. Note the stone bridges in Glen Tanar - always a clue to the past importance of these ancient highways.

Landranger No. 44.

Pathfinder Nos. 257, 271, 284.

Dinnet

Aboyne

Glen Tanar

summit 710m

Fungle Road

summit 723m

24km 15m

Tarfside

Glen ——— Esk

The Fungle Road

Also known as the Forest of Birse Mounth, this joins the Firmounth Road at its southern end having left Aboyne on Deeside. The route proceeds via Birse Castle, where it links up with a public road at its mid-point.

Landranger No:-44.

Pathfinder Nos:-257, 271, 284.

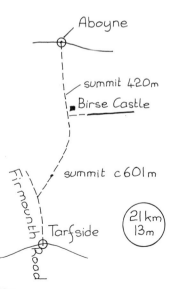

Aboyne

summit 420m

Birse Castle

Firmounth Road

summit c601m

21km 13m

Tarfside

Cairn o' Mount

Also Cairn a Mounth, and
the second Mounth road to
be improved to present-day
standards - now the B974
from Banchory to Fetter-
cairn. Like Cairnwell the
road is often closed due
to snow. There are
superb views south
from the summit
car park.

Landranger No:- 45.

Pathfinder Nos:- 258, 272,
                285.

The Builg Mounth

This route runs from
Strachan to Auchenblae
and is depicted on Doup
of Becky and Drumtochty
Forest. Despite the
afforestation the route can
be traced. Cyclists can divert
by enduring Hare Hill and via
Fetteresso Forest to circum-
navigate the path sections
of the true route.

Landranger No:- 45

Pathfinder Nos:- 258,
                272, 285.

138

The Stock Mounth

Another route starting
from Strachan, this time
by the eastern "leg"
of the Doup of Becky
tracks, the footpath
below Monluth Hill
and south via Bogton
on the Fetteresso
Forest tracks.

Landranger No:- 45.

Pathfinder Nos:- 258, 272.

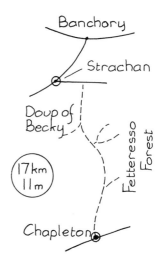

Cryne Corse Mounth

A route from Banchory
to Glenbervie which passes
through the heart of
Fetteresso Forest and
is indeed almost
smothered by trees
- in places the path
is little more than
a firebreak!

Landranger No:- 45.

Pathfinder Nos:- 258, 272.

Book 7 has been different; as much an exploration of the old highways as the glens - hence the inclusion of a special section giving a résumé of the main Mounth Roads. I am conscious that these roads deserve more thorough attention although the history of the region has already been expertly documented by others far more knowledgable than I. However, this guide cannot be a one-off and the 'glen' theme continues. In any event, in a weekend or holiday situation, exploring one glen or forest at a time is probably the most practical and enjoyable way for the individual to touch upon both landscape and history.... My wife and I are now impatient. We are craving for wilderness! Apart from Mount Keen and the central Monadhliath, we have not been able to truly lose ourselves in those vast tracts of land which take a couple of days to cross; and a week at a time in the wild just to begin to get to know. This has not happened since Book 3 - The Glens of Rannoch, but as I write plans are afoot (and awheel?) to explore just such a region. Book 8 will cover Morvern, Ardnamurchan, Sunart, Ardgour, Moidart, North and South Morar and ... best of all... Knoydart. Much will be on foot. We look forward to long days out in the wild. The very names conjour up visions of long, hard treks through the mountains and, hopefully, up quite a few of them while we are at it - if my readers will permit the odd day off! Yes, a generous dose of wilderness is overdue - our experience of the region up to now has been limited to road cycling, and gazing into those empty western glens from the roadside - a situation that must be put right without further delay!

Printed by
Carnmor Print & Design, London Road, Preston